HIDDEN HISTORY
of
NORTHEAST OHIO

Mark Strecker

THE
History
PRESS

Published by The History Press
Charleston, SC
www.historypress.com

Back cover: Rufus Putnam, Thomas Wightman and Thaddeus Mason Harris, "Map of the State of Ohio." *Courtesy of the Library of Congress.*

First published 2021

ISBN 9781467150682

Library of Congress Control Number: 2021943433

Notice: The information in this book is true and complete to the best of our knowledge. It is offered without guarantee on the part of the author or The History Press. The author and The History Press disclaim all liability in connection with the use of this book.

CONTENTS

CONTENTS

AUTHOR'S NOTE

A s anyone who has clicked on a broken link has discovered, websites have a habit of changing addresses, and it is for this reason that I have decided not to include web addresses for the places that appear in this book. The same is true about the price of entry fees for those locations that have them. These are subject to change, and once in print, they cannot be changed, even if the costs of the tickets do. I also figure that in the age of Google, looking up such information is faster than looking it up in a book.

PREFACE

There are many things about Northeast Ohio's past that I didn't know and probably wouldn't have learned had I not visited many of its museums and historical sites. It's this thrill of discovery that inspired this book, which explores a lesser-known place or topic in each of this region's counties. Before I could do that, I first needed to figure out which counties are located in Northeast Ohio—not as easy a task as I thought it would be, as geographers lack a consensus about which counties belong to the region. Some include just fourteen counties in their list, while others have up to twenty-two. I concluded that since Ohio has eighty-eight counties and one-fourth of that is twenty-two, twenty-two is the correct number.

Just because I chose a topic or place for a given county, that doesn't mean the events there didn't touch other counties. For example, for Columbiana County, I used the city of Salem to focus on the history of the abolitionist movement in Ohio, but it was hardly confined to this place. Medina County serves as the focal point to tell the story of the Lake Shore Electric Railway Company's interurban trolley system, which spanned from Cleveland to Toledo. Conversely, some of the history here is geographically specific. Packard Motor started in the city of Warren in Trumbull County. And the plot to liberate the Confederate prisoner of war camp on Johnson's Island could not have occurred in any other place but Erie County, just because that's where it was located.

During my research, I found so much material that this book was originally about twice its present length. Instead of saving the unused bits for another book or article, I decided to publish them on my website, www.markstrecker. com, in the form of travel logs. As a starting point for this project, I visited at least one museum or historical site in each of Northeast Ohio's counties, and the travel logs on my websites are about what I found. A complete list of these places can be found in the bibliography.

ACKNOWLEDGEMENTS

I would like to thank all of those working at the many museums and historical sites I visited for this book, as well as the various librarians who helped guide me to find difficult answers. Any mistakes made in this book are mine, not theirs. I especially want to thank Constance Ewazen, the president of the Historical Society of Old Brooklyn; David Stratton of the Salem Historical Society; Henry Halem, a tour guide at the Kent Historical Society Museum; Randolph S. Bergdorf, the director of Peninsular Library and Historical Society; and Olivia Hoge of the Cleveland Public Library.

I

ASHLAND COUNTY

The Destruction of Greentown

Near the town of Loudonville, there once stood a Native village known as Hell Town. Located on the Clear Fork branch of the Mohican River, it probably took its name from the German word for "clear" or "transparent." No one knows its precise location, though it's presumed to have stood somewhere on the southern line of what is now Green Township. Several Lenni-Lenape (Delaware) Natives—over whom were a couple notable chiefs, including Paxomet (Captain Thomas Steene Armstrong) and Kogiesch Quanoheel (Captain Pike)—lived there.

When Hell Town's inhabitants heard about the massacre of the peaceful Natives in the Moravian village of Gnadenhutten (which is about forty-six miles southeast of Loudonville as the crow flies), they skedaddled.* The Hell Town residents, along with some Mingo, Mohawk and a smattering of other Natives, established a new settlement called Greentown about three miles west of what is Perrysville today, on a bluff on the north bank of the Black Fork, a tributary of Mohican River. Located in the middle of alder marshes and on high ground, it was easily defended. Its inhabitants built about 150 pole huts.

The settlement was likely named after Thomas Green, whose murky history was brilliantly outlined in two articles by Peggy Mershon that appeared in the *Mansfield News Journal*. He was from Wyoming Valley in Pennsylvania, which stretches along the eastern bank of the Susquehanna

---

* For more information about Gnadenhutten, see chapter 21, Tuscarawas County: The Massacre at Gnadenhutten.

River and was once claimed by both Pennsylvania and Connecticut. Despite being a dedicated Tory, he inexplicably joined the American army on February 18, 1776, and deserted the next day. Perhaps he joined to get a bonus.

When the Revolutionary War broke out, the area was still a frontier, so its White settlers tried to gain the friendship or least pledged neutrality of its Native inhabitants. The British launched their own campaign of influence on the Native population. On July 3, 1778, a British lieutenant colonel, John Butler, led a contingent of rangers and Native allies to attack the Wyoming settlement. The incursion, known as the Battle of Wyoming Valley or the Wyoming Massacre, resulted in the deaths of 150 of the valley's settlers and forced the rest to surrender the forts they had built there. Although it was against the articles of war, after the surrender, the British and their Native allies plundered the settlers' property and destroyed their crops. Those who survived fled east, toward the Delaware River, or to Sunbury to the southwest.

Private Tom Green was one of those rangers. Earlier in the year, on February 12, he and Parshall Terry had led a raiding party of Mohawks to the Wyoming Settlement, culminating with the robbery of the house and property belonging to Amos York, whom they kidnapped, on February 14. After the war, Green, like many Tories, fled the then-independent United States for parts outside of its jurisdiction. It's thought that he may have married a Delaware woman. Though he was tied to Greentown's formation, after this, he disappeared from the historical record, leaving his ultimate fate unknown.

Paxomet served as Greentown's leader. About sixty-five years old at the time of its founding, Paxomet was a native of Pennsylvania and had lived somewhere along the Susquehanna River. Although he was not a full-blooded Native, this small man had dark skin, poor posture and two wives—one old and one young, both of whom bore him children. He also had two deaf servants from another tribe, probably captives. For several years, American settlers got along with Greentown's inhabitants. Among the settlement's closest friends was James Copus, a pious Methodist who preached in the village. Whether he was an ordained minister is unknown, but he had definitely been a hatter. Greentown's inhabitants trusted his honesty and integrity completely. Paxomet visited Copus's cabin frequently, especially in the spring, to acquire sugar made from maple sap.

Copus happened to be the first White settler in what would become Mifflin Township. Born in 1775 in Green County, Pennsylvania, he

Copyright, 1905, by John D. Morris & Company

THE WYOMING MASSACRE
Painting by F. O. C. Darley

The Wyoming Massacre. *Courtesy of the Library of Congress.*

married in that same place in 1796 and then emigrated to Ohio's Richland County in March 1809. He built temporary housing in the place where Charles Mill later appeared and that, at one point, was known as Zimmer's Run. Eighteen months later, he moved into a cabin on a high rocky bluff, located about one-fourth of a mile from the Mohican River's Black Fork. He cleared the land around his new cabin and planted corn. Of German stock, Copus was described by one source as stout and fearless. James Cunningham, Samuel and David Hill, Andrew Craig and John Lambright built their own houses nearby, and together, this little cluster became known as the Copus or Black Fork Settlement.

Tensions between the White settlers and Greentown's Native inhabitants rose with the outbreak of the War of 1812. The White settlers noticed that some of Greentown's residents, as well as those of another Native settlement called Jeromeville, made trips to Sandusky and returned amply supplied with blankets, ammunition and tomahawks. The possibility that these supplies had been provided by British agents stoked the Americans' fear that the British would make allies of the Native population. In August 1812, Colonel Samuel Kratzer of the U.S. Army ordered an officer named Captain Douglass to remove the people of Greentown to Piqua.

This violated the terms of the 1805 Treaty of Fort Industry, which granted all land west of the Cuyahoga River in the top third of Ohio to the Seneca, Wyandot, Shawnee, Munsee and Lenape. In exchange for giving up their lands to the east, the Natives received $1,000 a year in perpetuity. Settlers such as Copus were squatters. Captain Douglass had no business moving Native people anywhere, and the inhabitants of Greentown knew it.

To make things easier, Douglass asked Copus to help him with his task, hoping Copus could convince the villagers to leave willingly. Although Copus opposed their removal, a desire to avoid bloodshed prompted him to agree. In exchange for his help, he got Douglass to guarantee that as long as the people of Greentown surrendered, no harm would come to them or their property. Copus did his part, and the villagers left. As they disappeared into the forest, several stranglers from Douglass's command burned the village to the ground. So far as is known, no army officer ordered this. It is likely that these men did this as an act of revenge, as they themselves or their loved ones had suffered at the hands of Natives. When the Greentown villagers saw the smoke, they were infuriated. Copus was both distressed and surprised.

The next month, nineteen-year-old Philip Zimmer, the son of Frederick Zimmer, was tending to cows along a creek when he saw a group of Native warriors. He ran, but they assured him they just wanted to talk. They asked if his parents were home. After confirming that they were, the warriors departed. Alarmed, Philip ran to the Zimmers' hired man, Martin Ruffner, and reported his encounter. Ruffner told Philip to go to Copus, who lived about two miles to the south, to ask for help; he then got on his horse and galloped to the Zimmers' house.

Philip had two elderly parents and a sister, Catherine. Ruffner arrived before the warriors, whose number was between four and eight. At first, they acted perfectly friendly, so they were invited to dinner. After the food was ready, but before sitting down, they attacked. Ruffner shot one Native with his rifle and then used it as a club to knock another down. When his stock got lodged in a joint, the warriors responded with two shots and a tomahawk strike, killing him. They dragged his body outside and scalped him. At some point, possibly during the brief fight, several of Ruffner's fingers were cut off.

Catherine fainted at the sight of this. When she awoke, she watched the warriors strike her parents down, causing her to faint once more. Upon recovering for a second time, she shrieked and cried out, but the warriors weren't moved. They forced her to give them the family money and valuables and then grabbed a ring off her finger. The leader of this band, Kanotche, sank his tomahawk into her skull. She crumpled, dead, before the hearth. All three Zimmers lost their scalps.

Philip made his way to Copus's cabin and then went to retrieve John Lambright. The three reached the Zimmer cabin early in the evening. Ominously, no light shone from it. Copus cautiously crept inside, and, feeling his way, put his hand in a pool of blood. He told his companions what he had found. Ruffner was found in the yard. Copus prevented Philip from looking into the cabin, but when he returned later with reinforcements from Jacob Beam's blockhouse and Rocky Run, he saw the horror.

A military company from Wooster, led by a Captain Muller and Alex McConnel from New Philadelphia, tracked the perpetrators to Fern Island in the Tuscarawas River. Although the island was protected by a thick forest that made it quite secluded, Muller swam his horse to the island and took the fugitives by surprise. His men wanted to execute their prisoners immediately, but Muller insisted they get a fair trial. They were taken to New Philadelphia, where they were put into a jail. Kanotche claimed the motive had been robbery, not revenge. He refused to name his comrades, none of whom confessed.

Great excitement gripped Wooster when news of the family's murder arrived. Upon his return there, Muller reversed his earlier decision and decided to march his company to New Philadelphia with the intent of killing the prisoners. Tuscarawas County sheriff Henry Laffer called on the town's citizens to protect the prisoners, but they refused. Alex McConnel and John C. Wright, an attorney from Steubenville who happened to be in town, volunteered to help Laffer protect the prisoners.

When the militia arrived, the three pleaded for the lives of the prisoners and declared that if they were harmed, it would be over their dead bodies. Not willing to go that far, the Wooster company gave up and went home. The prisoners were held until Governor Return J. Meigs Jr. arrived. He turned the prisoners over the military, and Lieutenant Shane from the regular army took them to the western part of the state. During this trip, it is said two of the prisoners' escorts tried to buy poison to murder their charges. Considered prisoners of war by the army, the Natives were eventually released without suffering any consequences for what they'd done.

Frightened by the incident, Copus moved his family to the protection of a nearby blockhouse. A few days later, he decided to take his family home.

Soldiers accompanied him to serve as guards. On the morning of September 15, 1812, four of them went to a spring to wash themselves, leaving their arms behind. Just then, over forty-five Native warriors attacked. Three of the soldiers ran for Copus's cabin. The fourth, Robert Warnock, ran in the other direction. John Tedrick and George Shipley lost their lives and scalps. Warnock's body was later found about half a mile away. As Robert Dye passed between a shed and the cabin, a warrior stuck at him with his tomahawk, but Dye dodged the blow and made it to the house, though he had been hit twice by bullets. When the cabin door opened, Copus appeared with a rifle and shot one warrior, dead, but he took a bullet to the chest.

Copus urged his family and the soldiers within his cabin not to give up. His wife and daughter went up to the loft for safety while the others fought back. One of the soldiers inside the house, George Launtz, removed a chuck of wood from the cabin's wall to give him a place to poke his gun through. Before he did so, a ball came through and hit his arm, breaking it. Undaunted, he positioned his rifle, and when one of the warrior's poked his head above a stump, he blew the man's brains out.

The firefight lasted anywhere between half an hour and five hours. Sources do not tell us who else was in the house or how many of those who fought were soldiers or Copus children. In the end, the attackers gave up, picked up their dead and departed with many of Copus's sheep. Copus did not survive. The rest in the house did. It is likely the warriors had targeted Copus for what they perceived as his betrayal at Greentown.

After this incident, a messenger was dispatched to get reinforcements from the blockhouse. Along the way, this messenger came across a woodsman, James Chapman, who immediately went through the countryside, warning settlers of the attack. Chapman is known better to history as Johnny Appleseed. He often wore sackcloth shirts and either went barefooted or donned worn-out shoes. He was known for his kindness to animals, even rattlesnakes, which lived in Ohio at the time. Despite his nickname, his primary reason for living in the Northwest Territory wasn't to plant apple trees; rather, he was there to do missionary work. He aimed to spread the message of Swedish theologian Emanuel Swedenborg, a man who absolutely no one—save specialists in Protestant theologians—has heard of. Chapman planted apple trees out of self-interest. A good businessman, he planted seedlings in locations where pioneers were likely to settle so that he could sell them apples. After all, he had to eat, and he needed some sort of income, as his missionary work paid nothing.

When the War of 1812 ended, Ohio's Native people still possessed about one-sixth of the land in the state's northwest region. At this time, an estimated 2,500 Native people, including the Mingo, Lenape, Ottawa, Seneca, Shawnee and Wyandot, lived in villages along the Sandusky River and upper part of the Maumee River, as well as its tributaries. Still greedy for land, the United States launched an effort to buy the remaining portions of land belonging the Natives. Michigan's territorial governor Lewis Cass convinced Ohio's tribes (and a few from Michigan) to sell all—save some small portions—of their land in return for annual payments. This was codified in the 1827 Treaty of Fort Meigs.

Those Native people who remained decided to farm what land they had left. Adapting to the new reality around them, many prospered. Then Andrew Jackson was elected president, and everything changed. He wanted all Natives east of the Mississippi River moved to the river's western side, and in April 1830, a bill that became known as the Indian Removal Act was introduced in Congress that would give him the authority to do just that.

To their credit, Ohio senators Jacob Burnet and Benjamin Ruggles opposed the bill. Ruggles had been a member of the Democratic-Republican Party but switched to the Whig Party because he disliked Jackson. Burnet, who had moved from New Jersey to Cincinnati in 1790, felt that those Natives who had turned into peaceful farmers ought to be able to stay. The bill passed twenty-eight to nineteen. In the House of Representatives, only two of Ohio's fourteen representatives, James Shields and James Findlay, voted against the bill. After the bill was passed, Jackson signed it into law, forcing Ohio's remaining Native people to head west. To this day, Ohio has not one Native reservation, and as of 2019, a mere 0.3 percent of Ohioans identify as Native.

2

ASHTABULA COUNTY

The Ashtabula Train Disaster of 1876

On the night of December 29, 1876, a terrible snowstorm with winds of about sixty miles per hour roared through Ashtabula County. At the Lake Shore & Michigan Southern Railroad's depot, telegraph operator Wilham Asell got tired of waiting for the late *Pacific Express*—train no. 5—so he became determined to slog his way to his hotel. As he approached a crossing, he saw a headlamp coming around a curve and decided to wait for a moment to see if it belonged to a freight or passenger train. It being the latter, he turned around and started for the depot when a crashing sound stopped him. Looking back, he was horrified to see the lights of coaches disappearing into the gulch below. Stunned, he stood there for about two or three minutes.

Two men from the depot passed him on their way to investigate and asked him to come along. This suggestion broke his acute shock. He rushed to the gulch and was astounded to discover that the bridge was gone. He thought the engine had jumped the track. The three couldn't climb down into the gully because of its steepness, so they rolled down, which rendered one of Asell's arms useless. On the frozen river, Asell and the others began breaking windows in the carriages to get survivors out. One woman with an excessive girth got stuck while trying to squeeze through a window. Responding to her cry, Asell and others pulled her out, ripping her right out of her clothes.

Fires that were caused by upturned coal stoves broke out. These fires took many lives and left some victims burned beyond recognition. About twenty minutes to half an hour after the wreck occurred, Ashtabula's fire

Lake Shore & Michigan Railroad's engines 4704 and 4051. These are not the engines that fell into the gully, but they do present a good example of the type of engine the company used. *Courtesy of the Library of Congress.*

department arrived with its steam-powered engine and hose. Inexplicably, no water was thrown down into the gully. A coroner's jury later determined that the firemen had panicked, and had they acted rationally, they could've done something.

Those passengers who survived the wreck reported harrowing stories. Charles Carter had been playing cards in the palace car with three others when he heard breaking glass; then he said he felt the train falling. Seated with his back to the car's front, he got very quiet and held on. The impact seemed to cause him no harm, but one of his fellow cardplayers died instantly. Another, Mr. Shepard, suffered a broken leg. Worse, the car caught fire. Carter helped Shepard out, went back in to assist a woman and then returned for her young daughter. He later discovered he was covered in bruises. Shepard's leg was so badly broken that it had to be amputated.

The Bennett family was travelling from New York State to Jefferson, Ohio. The mother and father managed to get out. Their two children, one of them seriously injured, survived the ensuing fire, as someone tossed them over a pile of burning wood and into the arms of an unidentified man. The next morning, the mother gave birth, an event hastened by the trauma. Of the 159 people on board, 88 died immediately, and two expired later; 8 walked away unhurt. The last living thing to be extracted from the train was a bull terrier, whose cries resembled a human's. E.J. Griffin saved the pooch by opening a hole in the side of the car with a spike hammer.

When the light of day arrived, at least a dozen bodies could be seen. The cleanup and removal the remains of those who had died was slow going. The water, about three feet deep, needed to be dragged to find the rest of the missing passengers. The next day, a special train from Cleveland arrived with the surgeon of the road and his assistants to tend to the wounded, most of whom had been taken to the two hotels closest to the station. Beds were set up and put anywhere that room could be found, including in parlors, dining rooms and offices. Those who could be safely moved were put into the special train's sleeping car, a task made difficult by the snow and intense cold.

That same day, a coroner's jury assembled to investigate what had happened. It found that as the *Pacific Express* passed over the gully to reach the station on the other side at either 7:30 p.m. or 8:00 p.m. (sources vary), the bridge gave way, causing most of the train to crash into the dark abyss below. Its first engine, called the *Socrates* and driven by engineer Dan McGuire, made it safely to the other side. The second, the *Columbia*, driven by Gustav "Pap" Folsom, was less lucky. It plunged sixty-nine feet into the Ashtabula River below, taking with it the seven cars it pulled.

The bridge, which spanned 157 feet, had been built just eleven years earlier at an estimated cost of $75,000. Its parts had been produced in Cleveland. The jury determined it had collapsed due to defects and poor construction—something no inspecting engineer could possibly have missed. This was willful neglect by the Lake Shore & Michigan Southern Railroad. The fires could have been avoided if safety heaters, which were available, had been used. Safety heaters pumped steam into cars via a pipe connected car to car by a universal coupler.

The Ohio General Assembly formed its own special joint committee to investigate. This committee consisted of five members from the house and three from the senate. Assembled on January 12, 1877, it arrived at the scene on January 16 to interview witnesses and railroad officials. One of these officials was Charles Collins, the line's chief engineer and purchasing agent. The bridge was his responsibility. He told the committee that he didn't have the plans for that bridge, nor had he ever seen them. At the time of its construction, he had been overseeing another project. He didn't inspect the bridge himself—subordinates did that. The man who had done so, G.M. Reed, verbally told Collins that the bridge was fine, save for his discovery that the braces had been put on backwards. These were fixed, and more braces were added. Collins didn't use that as an excuse to escape his ultimate responsibility. Guilt over the incident led him to commit suicide.

It was the Lake Shore & Michigan Southern Railroad's own president, Amasa Stone, who had overseen the bridge's construction. Stone was an experienced bridge builder whose career began in 1839. The first bridge he ever worked on spanned the Connecticut River, which was later destroyed by a flood in 1846. He was asked to construct its replacement. By the time the Lake Shore & Michigan Southern Railroad came into being, he had largely removed himself from business, as he had been devastated by the death of his only son, Adelbert Barns, who drowned in 1868. Nonetheless, "Commodore" Cornelius Vanderbilt and other Lake Shore & Michigan Southern Railroad stockholders convinced Stone to become the railroad's managing director. Ohio's joint committee determined that the Ashtabula bridge had collapsed due to poor design and defects that should have been detected. The committee, lacking police power, created a regulatory bill for bridges and their inspection in Ohio.

This wreck was no outlier in the American railroad industry in the nineteenth century. Railroads were simply unsafe for workers and riders. In 1888, the Interstate Commerce Commission tabulated reports from the nation's railroads and found that 315 passengers had died, 2,138 passengers had been injured, 2,070 employees had been killed and 20,148 employees had been hurt. A further breakdown of employee injuries and deaths found that brakemen were especially vulnerable. The Brotherhood of Railroad Brakemen had an average of just over 10,000 members, but this number fluctuated due, in part, to the staggering number of deaths and permanent disabilities its members suffered.

3

CARROLL COUNTY

The Fighting McCooks

D aniel McCook moved to Carroll County's Carrollton in 1832. During the twenty-one years he and his family lived there, they had a profound impact on both the town and the county in which it's located. Daniel and his two brothers, John and George, produced a considerable extended family. John and his wife, Catherine, raised five sons and one daughter: Edward Moody, Anson George, Henry Christopher, Roderick Sheldon, John James and Mary Gertrude. George Jr. and his wife, Margret, produced just one child, George Latimer; but Daniel and his wife, Martha, outdid them all with twelve children: (in order of birth dates) Latimer A., George Wythe, John James, Catherine, Robert Latimer, Mary Jane, Alexander McDowell, Daniel Jr., Edwin Stanton, Martha, Charles Morris, and, finally, John James, whose older brother and namesake had died at the age of nineteen in 1842 of a disease he picked up during a South American training expedition with the navy. The McCook family become known as the "Fighting McCooks," as, during the Civil War, fifteen men from their extended family served in some capacity, four of them dying during that conflict.

In 1790, the family's patriarch, George McCook, came to America, not to find a better life, but to escape British authorities. Of Scottish descent, McCook was born in Ballymoney, Ireland, in 1752, and as a young adult, he joined an Irish independence group known as the United Irish. When it launched a failed rebellion, British authorities came for its members, prompting George, along with his wife and nine-year-old daughter, Fanny, to flee to America. Finding the East Coast too expensive, the family moved to a place near Pittsburgh. Deciding the danger of attacks from Natives was too great a risk, McCook relocated to Canonsburg in Pennsylvania's Chartiers Valley, where he became a merchant.

George and his wife produced five more children. Planning to marry off his three daughters to prosperous men, McCook aimed to make his sons into gentlemen, insisting they became doctors, lawyers or ministers. With that in mind, McCook supported the founding of Jefferson College in Canonsburg, the first institution of higher learning west of the Appalachian Mountains. His sons did as they were told. George Jr., born in 1795, became a doctor. Daniel, born in 1798, became a lawyer. John, born in 1806, became a doctor and businessman. In 1819, George Jr. and his wife, Margaret Latimer, moved to New Lisbon, Ohio. John and his wife, Catherine Julia Sheldon, followed. Daniel and his wife, Martha Latimer, moved there in 1824.

Daniel brought with him a brass cannon that was used in the War of 1812 and that had stood outside of the Black Horse Tavern as a souvenir from this conflict. Both Canonsburg and Daniel claimed ownership of the cannon, the latter saying it had come with the Black Horse when he purchased it in 1819. Upon moving to Lisbon, Daniel had the cannon smuggled out of town in one of his wagons. For this, he was arrested, but a court determined that his ownership was valid.

When the construction of the Sandy and Beaver Canal was proposed in 1828 and Daniel realized its route from Bolivar, Ohio, to Beaver,

Daniel McCook's home in Carrolton is now the McCook House Civil War Museum. *Photograph taken by the author.*

Pennsylvania, went right through the land that he and his brother George Jr. owned, Daniel went to Columbus to convince the Ohio General Assembly to create a new county to encompass the canal. After a bit of bribery to get the last vote that was needed (Daniel was sometimes ethically challenged), Carroll County was created. Its capital was to be Carrollton, named for Charles Carroll of Carrollton, Maryland; at the time, he was the oldest living signer of the Declaration of Independence.

Daniel had a house built in Carrollton made of bricks from the brickyard he'd established. In addition to this house, he co-owned several local mills and speculated in land. He hoped to use the canal to ship his grain and wool interests to New Orleans and New York City. In addition to being a businessman and lawyer, Daniel also dabbled in politics. In Columbiana County, he'd been elected treasurer, and in Carroll County, he served as the clerk of courts.

In 1836, George Jr. decided to run as the Democratic candidate for a U.S. representative seat in Ohio's Seventeenth District. The Whigs ran Andrew W. Loomis. Loomis earned more votes in Carroll County than George Jr., so Daniel, in his capacity as the clerk of courts, declared his brother the winner by deceptively giving 837 votes to "Andrew W. Loomis" and the other 116 to "Andrew Loomis." This plot failed to work. Loomis still won the district.

This violation of the law didn't go unanswered. The Whigs impeached Daniel. His defense lawyer, family friend Edwin Stanton, had to represent his client on the sly because, at the time, he was running for prosecutor in Jefferson County and didn't want the fact that he was defending someone for voter fraud to get out. A grand jury packed with Democrats managed to delay the trial for several sessions, giving Democratic operatives a chance to find some dirt on the Whigs. When it was discovered that the Whigs had illegally used party funds to pay for their trip to a political convention, the Democrats charged them with malfeasance. At a draw, both matters were dropped. It is doubtful that Daniel felt any contrition, as, in November 1844, he got in trouble again. This time, the elders of his church, Carrollton Presbyterian, accused him of betting $50,000 on the outcome of the presidential election. He pled guilty.

The thing that had motivated Daniel to found Carroll County, the Sandy and Beaver Canal, was a dud. It took workers from 1834 to 1848 to dig the canal in its entirety with a length under what was first proposed. In 1837, two floods silted parts of the canal up and blocked the entrance of Big Tunnel. In that same year, the canal's director and prime mover, William Christmas, died. Then came the Panic of 1837, which halted further major construction for the next seven years. By the time the canal opened in 1846, the railroads had rendered it obsolete. On April 12, 1852, the Cold Run Reservoir collapsed and destroyed parts of the canal; it was a catastrophe that fortunately resulted in no deaths, as Judge John Bowman had noticed a leak and warned everyone of the reservoir's impending failure. The canal continued to operate until 1884, when key parts of its infrastructure were destroyed by flooding.

After the railroad failed to pass through Carroll County or New Lisbon, Daniel decided to invest his time and money elsewhere. In 1847, he mortgaged eighteen properties—his house among them—and steamed down the Ohio River to southern Illinois, where he purchased 2,360 acres of land laden with iron ore that he planned to mine and sell to the railroads that were heading west. In Elizabeth, Illinois, Daniel started Martha Furnace to smelt the ore. There, he built a house at a cost of $10,000.

Daniel's son George Wythe fought in the Mexican-American War. Born in Canonsburg in 1821, he served with the Third Ohio Regiment and became its commander. During his service, he contracted malaria, one of the world's most pernicious mosquito-transmitted diseases—not a pleasant thing to have. Its symptoms include chills, fever and sweating. Worse, even after recovery, the disease sometimes sticks around and can reoccur up to thirty years later. No cure exists; though, in George Wythe's lifetime, it was known that the bark of the cinchona tree from Peru, from which quinine is derived, relieved malaria's symptoms. After the war, George returned to Steubenville, where he and his partner, Edward Stanton, had a law office.

When the Civil War broke out, George aimed to fight and took a commission as a brigadier general. To this, his long-suffering wife, Margaret, objected. He was nearly forty years old and still suffering from bouts of malaria. The couple had three young children, and Margaret's health was fragile. When none of her pleading seemed to work, she cried. Fine—he would go to Columbus and decline the position. While he was there, George was asked to lead troops to Washington, D.C., as it appeared to be in imminent danger of being invaded. This he did. Upon his return, he became an adjunct general, or a general who does administrative work focused on the wellbeing and combat readiness of troops. In 1871, he started a run for Ohio's governorship on the Democratic ticket, but ill health caused him to drop out. The next year, he died.

John's son Edward Moody was born in Steubenville in 1833, and he pursued law and politics. Having a bit of wanderlust, in 1849, Edward moved to Minnesota. Ten years, later he headed to Colorado as part of the

Major General Edward M. McCook. *Courtesy of the Library of Congress.*

Pike's Peak gold rush. There, he settled in Central City and, unlike most there, made a small fortune, probably as a practicing lawyer and not from prospecting. Before the Civil War, he served for a time as a secret agent in Washington, D.C.

During the Civil War, Edward distinguished himself as a deliverer of dispatches for General Winfield Scott through the Confederate lines in Maryland. For this, he was made first lieutenant in the calvary, which took him to Tennessee, where he became good friends with his commanding officer, Ulysses S. Grant. Edward achieved the rank of brigadier general, commanding men of the Army of the Cumberland. At the siege of Atlanta, his men prevented General John B. Hood, the man in charge of the Confederates in the city, from receiving reinforcements, forcing him to abandon the city.

After the war, Edward briefly served as the military governor of Florida. Later, he became the minister to the Sandwich Islands, now Hawaii. In 1869, President Grant appointed him governor of the Colorado Territory. While he was busy working to expand the territory's economy and attract new settlers, Edward and his brother-in-law James B. Thompson were accused of lining their pockets with $22,000 from a government contract that was supplying the Utes with sheep and cattle. Grant removed Edward from his post in 1873, when the controversy became too much.

Unwilling to allow his reputation to be tarnished, Edward headed straight to Washington, D.C., to clear his name. Grant, a notoriously bad judge of character, took Edward's word that he was innocent and restored him to his governorship. This sparked Republican infighting in the territory, and in an effort to maintain party unity, Grant once again removed his friend. Edward, nonetheless, remained in Colorado the rest of his life.

Charles Morris, Daniel's son, refused to accept an officer's commission and instead enlisted as a private in the Second Ohio Volunteer Infantry, which soon participated in the First Battle of Bull Run. When war broke out, the head of the U.S. Army, General Winfield Scott, knew his force wasn't ready for a fight, so instead, he suggested to President Lincoln that he implement a slow strangulation of the South via a blockade. Public sentiment made Scott's long-term Anaconda Plan unacceptable, so Lincoln ordered General Irvin McDowell to march on Richmond. The Confederacy appointed General Pierre G.T. Beauregard to stop this force. At the resulting First Battle of Bull Run, the Union's initial success was thwarted by General Thomas J. Jackson, whose force's immovability gave him the nickname Stonewall Jackson. This delay gave the Confederate reinforcements under

A. Pfott., *First Battle of Bull Run. Courtesy of the Library of Congress.*

General Joseph E. Johnston time to arrive and push the Union forces into a retreat back to Washington, D.C.

During the battle, Charles came across his father, Daniel, who had volunteered as a nurse, working with the wounded. Charles stopped to help. As he set out to rejoin his company, he was surrounded by an officer and several troopers of the Confederate's Black Horse Cavalry. When the cavalry's men asked Charles to surrender, he refused. He disabled an officer with his musket and then kept them at bay with his bayonet. The Rebels shot him, leaving him to die in his father's arms.

Daniel lost another son, Robert Latimer, the next year. Born in Columbiana County in 1827, Robert had trained as a lawyer before the war at his brother's practice in Steubenville; he then moved to Columbus for a time. In Cincinnati, he formed the partnership of Stallo & McCook. He developed a close relationship with the city's German population, so when the Civil War broke out, they asked him to become colonel of a regiment they were raising, the Ninth Ohio. Knowing nothing about the military, he agreed and learned his new trade from the regiment's experienced officers. The Germans had asked him to become their colonel because they knew a born-and-bred American at the regiment's head would avoid any unpleasantness with the fact that many of the regiment's men spoke no English.

At Camp Dennison, located in the city, Robert made sure his regiment had everything it needed. This boosted moral, and as a result, his well-drilled men all reenlisted for three more years. Other regiments were not so well-equipped, and Robert's success at outfitting his own regiment was, no doubt, due to his personal clout and connections. After all, his brother Edward was the former law partner of Secretary of War Stanton, and he had worked for the man. Robert affectionately called the regiment his "Bully Dutchmen." When he was made a brigadier general in Buell's army, he made sure his former regiment was part of that.

In Tennessee, Robert came down with dysentery. Surgeons told him he needed to go to Nashville to recover, but he refused to leave his troops, despite the fact he could not sit up. So, they put him on a cot and carted him around in an ambulance. On August 5, 1862, while heading from Athens, Alabama, to Decherd, Tennessee, Robert and a few men went looking for a good place to encamp. While doing so, Confederate guerrillas surrounded the ambulance. Robert—or rather the wagon carrying him—tried to escape, but when it was clear that escape was impossible, Robert surrendered. One of the Confederate officers, Captain Frank Gurley, fired three shots at them, one of which hit Robert in the side. He died the next day.

Robert Latimer McCook. *Courtesy of the Library of Congress.*

A counternarrative written by an anonymous Confederate private who was there appeared in the January 1886 issue of *Southern Bivouac*. The private was from Huntsville, Alabama, and had enlisted in the company shortly after General Nathan Forrest commissioned Gurley to form it with the mandate of harassing the fifteen to twenty thousand Union troops north of the Tennessee River. The private witnessed Robert's death and aimed to tell the truth of the matter.

While operating along the Tennessee–Alabama border, the private's company received intelligence that a high-ranking Union officer was in the vicinity, traveling down Gum Spring Road with just four or five hundred cavalrymen guarding him. But when they caught up with the officer—it was General George A. Thomas—at his camp in Rock Spring, Alabama, they decided there were too many soldiers there to make an attempt to get him. The next morning, while skirmishing with Union troops at near New Market, Alabama, the company came across two enemy officers in a buggy (which was identified as a cart in another source, a more likely conveyance).

To induce the Union soldiers to stop, they fired at them, and it was then that Robert was hit. Captain Gurley moved the wounded McCook to a nearby house, where he died. No one in the company knew who had fired the fatal shot. Gurley did take Robert's sword, which had been presented to him by Congress. Gurley returned it to the family after the war. The anonymous private made it clear that Gurley didn't shoot Robert after his surrender.

It is probable that the private's account is closer to the truth, but it mattered little to the McCook family. To them, Gurley had outright murdered their kin, and for that, he had to pay. In early September 1863, Robert's brother Colonel Daniel McCook Jr. set up camp at Hurricane Creek, near Huntsville, Alabama, about a mile away from the farm where Gurley was raised. Daniel ordered Colonel J.T. Holmes to take fifty soldiers from the Fifty-Second Ohio to burn all the buildings there. With the exception of a couple of slaves' shacks, Holmes's men burned down twenty-five structures, including the house in which Gurley had been born.

On October 13, Captain Lawson Kilborn tracked a sick Gurley to his brother's house near Brownsboro, Tennessee. Gurley tried to escape out the back, but Kilborn had foreseen that and placed men on guard there. Once apprehended, Gurley should have been made a prisoner of war, but instead, he was tried and found guilty of murder. Although he was sentenced to death, President Lincoln never approved his execution. Gurley remained in the Tennessee State Penitentiary until the war's end.

After returning to Madison County, Tennessee, Gurley ran for and won the office of the sheriff. Upon learning of this, the McCooks used their political influence to have Gurley arrested. A military tribunal tried him, found him guilty and sentenced him to death for a second time. President Andrew Johnson put a hold on the execution and, after examining the evidence, freed Gurley, though Gurley never assumed his office.

On July 8, 1863, Brigadier General John Hunt Morgan led about 2,100 troops into Ohio, prompting the elder Daniel McCook to try to raise a force of mounted men to confront the raiders.

General John Hunt Morgan. *Courtesy of the Library of Congress.*

However, as McCook was unable to secure the needed horses, this effort went nowhere. Instead, he volunteered as a private in Major Tom Cook's force under the command of Brigadier General Henry M. Judah. Daniel, then sixty-six years old, didn't tell his wife about his enlistment until the day of his departure. Near Portsmouth, he heard that Gurley was among the men under Morgan's command. He informed General Judah that he would obey no order that prevented him from shooting Gurley, even if he was a prisoner of war.

On July 2, 1863, Morgan had led 2,460 men into Kentucky through the Cumberland Gap, then sent two companies ahead to steal boats for crossing the Ohio River. They captured two packet boats, the *Alice Dean* and *J.J. McCombs*. Deciding to circumvent the well-guarded city of Cincinnati, Morgan crossed into Indiana. As his force did so, the Union gunboat *Springfield* appeared but was chased off with Morgan's parrot guns, which had a farther range. The Indiana militia offered some resistance but not enough to stop the raiders. Once on the northern side of the river, the Confederates burned their boats and marched six miles inland. They remained in Indiana for five days, during which time, they stole horses and supplies from civilians.

By the time he crossed into Ohio, Morgan had fewer than two thousand men, the others having either been lost to skirmishes or failed to keep up with the rapid pace. He marched his men for thirty-five hours straight, covering about ninety miles in an effort to avoid getting caught near

Cincinnati, where Generals Judah and Ambrose Burnside had troops. During this nonstop trek, Morgan's only notable encounter was a skirmish against Union soldiers near Camp Dennison.

One Ohio newspaper, the *Newark Advocate*, treated the raid like a sporting event. A July 17, 1863 story reported, "When we last left the redoubtable John yesterday morning...his forces were crossing the Colerain Turnpike (twelve or fifteen miles north of Cincinnati) and were moving in the direction of Glendale and Springdale, both of which places his troops passed through, carrying off some of the finest horses of our suburban fellow citizens." Between Reading and Montgomery, Morgan's men visited the farm of Thomas Schneck to steal some of his best horses. "The splendid premium horse Tuckahoe, known to all who have visited the Hamilton County Fairs, didn't fancy a rebel rider and snapped at him so mischievously and deported himself otherwise so uninviting that Mr. Rebel left him."

Morgan's men took some peculiar loot; bolts of calico were a favorite. One man carried with him three canaries in their cage for two days before abandoning them. Another put a chafing dish designed to look like a coffin on his saddle's pummel until forced by an officer to toss it. In Piketon, a raider broke into a store and stuffed horn buttons into his pockets. Most raiders ultimately threw their useless prizes away. While the Confederates busied themselves with their looting, General Judah ordered two gunboats boats to patrol the Ohio River to prevent Morgan from crossing back over the river. Ohio's governor, David Tod, called out over fifty thousand militiamen to deal with the Confederate force.

On July 18, at eight in the evening, Morgan arrived in Portland to ford the river, then unseasonably high, to reach Buffington Island, from which he planned to cross the rest of the river to reach West Virginia on the other side. Portland offered a hastily constructed earthwork with Union soldiers behind it. With his horses and men tired, Morgan decided to wait until the morning make an attempt at overrunning the defenses.

About then, General Judah arrived with a small force to recontour the land. The Confederates unleashed a volley into this force, causing some men to panic, many making their way to the river and scrambling around the one piece of artillery they brought, a caisson. About twenty Union men were killed or wounded, Daniel McCook being among the latter. As the Confederates took forty to fifty prisoners; Judah led the rest to safety. Hit in the spine and side, Daniel was put onto a steamer headed for Cincinnati, but he died before reaching the city. Gurley had never been part of Morgan's force.

The arrival of 2,800 Union cavalrymen under General Edward Hobson forced Morgan and approximately 1,200 of his men to escape northward. At another ford north at Reedsville, about 300 raiders got across before gunboats under the command of Leroy Fish arrived to prevent the remaining 900 from going any farther. Judah's full force of 1,100, in combination with Hobson's men, chased after Morgan, who found all the fords guarded by artillery, gunboats and sharpshooters. In his last attempt to cross, about 150 of his men drowned.

Those who remained with him managed to elude capture and make their way about 170 miles northward. But here were two more Union forces—one from Michigan under the command of General William T.H. Brooks, and one from Pennsylvania under the command of Major W.B. Way. Suspecting Morgan would come up the road that went through Salineville, Brooks set up his headquarters in nearby Wellsville at a Cleveland & Pennsylvania Railroad depot to monitor the situation, no doubt using the telegraph. Brooks also set troops up in Salineville to confront Morgan if he came.

On July 26, Morgan's force arrived. Upon seeing the Union soldiers ahead, Morgan's men tried to turn around and flee, but Major Way's men were coming at him from behind. A short fight ensued. Morgan tried to escape in a carriage drawn by two white horses, but Major Way saw him and stopped it. Morgan leaped out the other side, jumped over a fence, stole a horse and then led 364 of his men away. They were soon surrounded and captured by a cavalry force under the command of Major G.W. Rue.

Morgan became a guest at the Ohio State Penitentiary in Columbus. On November 26, 1863, he and six officers escaped by digging a tunnel into an airshaft using table knives. Morgan rejoined the Confederate army, and the next year, he led yet another raid into Kentucky, one with much less success compared to his earlier forays. In September 1864, he led a raiding party into a pro-Union part of eastern Tennessee, and near Knoxville, he launched a surprise attack against Union forces. At Greeneville, he and his men were surrounded, and when he tried to flee through a garden, a Union private shot him in the back.

4

COLUMBIANA COUNTY

Salem and the Ohio Abolitionist Movement

S alem was quite progressive in the nineteenth century, with such milestones as having its first female doctor, Elizabeth Grizell, open her practice in the 1840s, long before this became the norm. The city's openminded character was probably a result of it being settled by the Religious Society of Friends, or the Quakers, pacifists who greatly valued education and were no strangers to being ahead of their time. Zadok Street, a retired New Jersey clockmaker, and John Straughan, a pottery maker from Pennsylvania, founded the town on April 30, 1806. The Western Anti-Slavery Society had its headquarters there—not a surprise, considering the Quakers fervently opposed slavery.

One of the most important buildings in town that was tied to the antislavery movement and the Underground Railroad was Liberty Hall. Built in 1840, the lower floor served as Sam Reynolds's carpenter shop, and its upper floor served as the meeting place for Western Anti-Slavery Society. It was there that the town's Quaker population discussed helping enslaved people escape to freedom via the Underground Railroad. It was also from Liberty Hall, on August 28, 1854, that a group of Salem abolitionists plotted to rescue an enslaved girl. It just so happened that the twentieth anniversary of the Western Anti-Slavery Society was meeting in Salem at the time. At about 4:00 p.m. during that day's session, someone announced that they had received a telegram that an enslaved girl was going to be on a train that was arriving at 6:00 p.m. from the east. Who would defend the principles they espoused? Quite a few headed to the train station.

This replica of Liberty Hall, called Freedom Hall, was built by the Salem Historical Society Museum. *Photograph taken by the author.*

When the train arrived, Daniel Howell Hise, Benjamin Bown, Abram Brooke, Doctor Thomas and a Mr. Blackwell from Cincinnati approached the girl's master and asked if she was enslaved. Yes, and he was her owner. They informed him they were taking her with them. The enslaved girl's owner's wife shrieked bloody murder and cursed the men out—but to no avail. Realizing he wouldn't win, the girl's master handed over her clothes. According to the account published by Frederick Douglass in the newspaper that bore his name, the girl, who was between the ages of ten and twelve, desired to stay with her mistress, probably because she considered her mistress a surrogate mother. Douglass reported that it wasn't a member of the Western Anti-Slavery Society who grabbed her; rather, it was some bystanders who were unaffiliated with that group who planned to get a writ of habeas corpus to secure her freedom.

That evening, the abolitionists discussed what should be done with the rescued girl. They raised fifty dollars to cover the cost of her clothing and education, and then they named her Abby Kelly Salem. What her original name was or why she had no say in choosing her new one is not recorded in any the historical records. The girl's first and middle name were a tribute to pioneering abolitionist Abigail Kelley Foster, the Quaker whose speeches changed the minds of many about slavery.

Somewhat forgotten by history, Foster left her teaching career in 1839 to preach against the evils of slavery. This didn't go down well with many ministers, who called her a "Jezebel," "a very bad woman" and an agent of Satan. Politicians called her a "man's woman." Born Abby Kelley on January 15, 1811, in the Massachusetts village of Pelham, Foster's lack of popularity possibly had to do with the fact that her father had come from Ireland in an era when the Irish were hated by many Americans. Undaunted by having people toss rotten eggs, feces and bottles at her, Foster continued to make public speeches about the cause she fervently believed in.

Abby Kelley Foster. *Courtesy of the Library of Congress.*

Foster had probably made an impression on the good people of Salem ten years earlier when she spoke for three days to mostly Quakers and some Black residents at the Western Anti-Slavery Society's annual meeting in nearby New Lisbon. There, she suggested that the people of Ohio needed their own antislavery newspaper, as the two major antislavery newspapers from the east, the *Liberator* and the *Standard*, took anywhere between ten days and two weeks to reach its subscribers in the state. Three months later, the first issue of the *Anti-Slavery Bugle* appeared. It was four pages in length and not well printed. Foster recognized that for this new periodical to survive, it needed subscribers, so she put her energy toward acquiring them. By April 1846, it had one thousand subscribers. Foster convinced Lizzie Hitchcock and Benjamin Jones to become the newspaper's first editors. They set up a permanent shop in Salem. The paper lasted for fifteen years.

Its stewardship was passed to Marius and Emily Robinson. Marius, who had been born in Dalton, Massachusetts, on July 26, 1806, had a somewhat unhappy childhood. Raised by strict Presbyterians, his doubts about being saved and worries over damnation caused him to go through fits of depression. At the age of ten, his family moved to Chautauqua County, New York, and at the age of fifteen, he had an epiphany that he was destined to do great work.

Unable to pay for his education, Marius's parents apprenticed him to the printing and bookbinding firm Merrill and Hastings in Utica. When his apprenticeship ended in 1827, Marius moved to Tennessee to attend Dr.

Isaac Anderson's Southern and Western Theological Seminary in Maryville. Next, he spent a year as an assistant at a Presbyterian church in Florence, Alabama, and then he returned to school for further training to become a minister at the University of Nashville. He completed the five-year course in just two years.

With his education still incomplete, Marius next studied at Lane Theological Seminary in Cincinnati. One of the school's professors, Theodore Weld, transformed his pupil into an ardent abolitionist, prompting Robinson and other students to give aid to Cincinnati's free Black population. The majority of the city's people had a southern view of race relations, and because the city's citizens found this unacceptable, they pressured the university's board of trustees to order its students to cease and desist. In protest, Robinson and forty fellow students left the school. Robinson joined the newly formed Ohio American Anti-Slavery Society (later called the Western Anti-Slavery Society) and aided in the publication of its newspaper, the *Philanthropist*. Located in Cincinnati, a mob stormed and wrecked the paper's office.

During his time in the city, Marius met Emily Rakestraw, who had come there to teach the city's Black population, and the two eventually married. Marius made public appearances to advocate for abolitionism for the Western Anti-Slavery Society and worked in Ohio. In early June 1837 in Berlin, an angry mob of about one dozen people dragged Marius from the house of Jesse Garretson, where he was staying as a guest, and took him to Canfield, beating, tarring and feathering him along the way.

Theodore Dwight Weld. *Courtesy of the Library of Congress.*

Although it sounds amusing today, this form public shaming was nothing less than torture. Not everyone survived the ordeal, and sometimes, those who did, like Marius, suffered from poor health afterward. The idea of tarring and feathering originated in New England. Most often, the tarring was done with hot pine tar, a thick black or brown liquid produced by boiling sap out of a mature pine tree placed over an open pit fire. It blistered the skin upon contact and, even if applied cold, was very difficult to get off. Turpentine would help, but it left already damaged skin even more irritated. Feathers were often poured on top of the victim from a pillow or two.

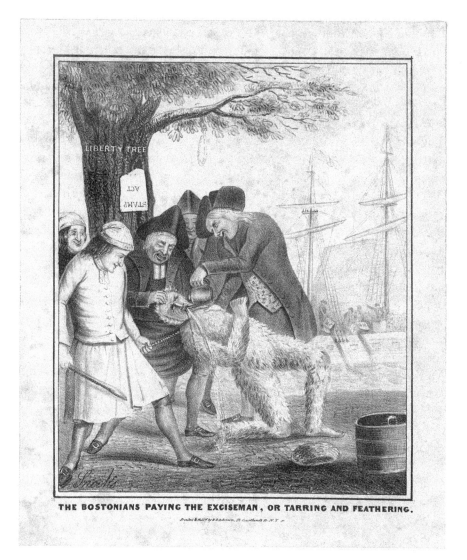

THE BOSTONIANS PAYING THE EXCISEMAN, OR TARRING AND FEATHERING.

Revolutionary-era illustration of tarring and feathering. *Courtesy of the Library of Congress.*

It took Marius a month to recover enough to resume his work, but he was still not ready and nearly lost his voice. For the next eight months, he stayed at home to recuperate. Again, he went out to lecture, but his voice gave out, and he resigned from his duties to spend the next ten years living in effective retirement from abolitionism and religion. In 1850, he returned to the antislavery movement by becoming the president of the Western Anti-Slavery Society in Salem.

That year, he took over the editorship of the *Anti-slavery Bugle*, and Emily became its publishing agent, though by 1859, he had quit due to his ill health. After Kelly Salem's rescue, an editorial appeared in the paper that said it didn't consider those who had taken her "mobocrats and violators of the law," as the girl had already been kidnapped by her former owners. It claimed Ohioans had a legal right to liberate any enslaved people they came across (they didn't) and a moral obligation to do so.

Interestingly, the *Bugle* also printed an unfavorable account of Abby's liberation that had appeared in the *Cleveland Leader*. In this version of events, "a big negro" accosted the girl's master and asked him if she was enslaved. When he said yes, it was said the Black man seized the girl against her will and took her despite the fact that she clung her mistress and begged not to be taken. Her liberator bruised the girl's mistress's neck in the process. The girl begged to be returned but to no avail. The girl's owner's life, this article claimed, was threatened. It noted that among those present was "that long-haired, brainless C.C. Burleigh."

Charles Calistus Burleigh did have long, blond hair (and an impressive beard), but brainless he was not. Born in Plainfield, Connecticut, on November 3, 1810, he traced his heritage back to William Bradford, the governor of the Plymouth Colony who had arrived on the *Mayflower*. Although he was trained as a lawyer, Burleigh dedicated his life to the antislavery movement and worked in it for the next thirty years. He vowed to never cut his hair until all enslaved people were free in the United States, but judging by a photograph of him from 1865, he may not have kept to that pledge. In addition to serving as a deacon at the Congregational Church of Plainfield and editing the *Unionist* newspaper, published out of Brooklyn, Connecticut, Burleigh was a renowned orator, and during the Abby Kelly Salem incident, he spoke persuasively to the crowd there.

He needed to speak because although Ohio was considered a free state, it was not uniformly antislavery. Those who lived north of the National Road, which consisted of about two-thirds of the state, tended to be antislavery, while those who settled south of the National Road didn't support antislavery, mainly because most of those who had settled in Ohio's bottom third had come from Kentucky. Ohio's government was also not especially enlightened about the treatment of its Black population. Those who wrote Ohio's first constitution initially allowed Black residents to become citizens, but this provision was later removed. In 1804, a year after Ohio became a state, it passed a law requiring Black settlers to present evidence of their freedom to the county clerk. Those with Black employees who were unable to prove their free status were fined. Failing to comply could result in a fine between $10 and $50. In 1807, a more draconian law forbade Black residents from staying in the state for more than twenty days unless they could secure a $500 bond signed by two free persons. The penalty for employing a Black person who was unable to prove their free status was increased to $100. Black residents were also forbidden from testifying in court against a White person.

In 1838, the state passed the Fugitive Slave Law that allowed slave catchers to apprehend and return escaped slaves to their masters. One example of its use occurred in 1842 in Fitchville, a village about sixteen miles southeast of Norwalk. There, twelve escapees, including men, women and children, were apprehended on a Sunday morning in early November. Chained, the escapees were placed on a guarded stagecoach. When it rolled through Norwalk during a time when many churches held their services, no one tried to stop it. Upon hearing about the stagecoach, a few outraged Norwalk citizens decided to buy the fugitives' freedom, and to that end, they

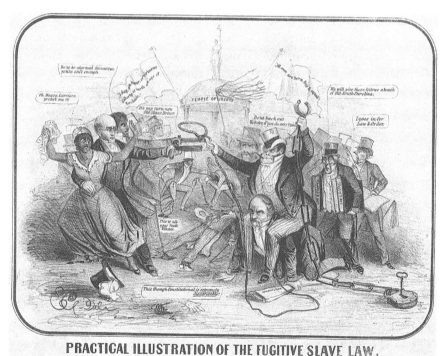

PRACTICAL ILLUSTRATION OF THE FUGITIVE SLAVE LAW.

Political cartoon commenting on the Fugitive Slave Act of 1850. *Courtesy of the Library of Congress.*

went to the courthouse to form a committee that would contact the owners in Kentucky. The next year, popular sentiment caused the Ohio General Assembly to repeal the Fugitive Slave Law. The state repealed most of its anti-Black laws in 1849.

When President Millard Fillmore signed the Fugitive Slave Act of 1850, it became illegal to aid and abet any escaped enslaved people in the United States and its territories. But by then, the Underground Railroad had become quite adept at keeping fugitives out of the hands of slave catchers—especially in Ohio. The state had multiple routes, and Salem was one of its largest stops. A brochure produced by the Salem Tourism Advisory Board, supplemented by a CD produced by the Salem Historical Society, lists twelve places in the town that either once hid enslaved people or housed prominent members of the Underground Railroad. These locations include the houses of Joel McMillan, whose family employed Abby Kelly Salem for many years, and Daniel Howell Hise, one of those who participated in Salem's liberation; the carpenter shop of Sam Reynolds, in which the decision to rescue Salem was made; and the home of Marius and Emily Robinson, who ran the *Anti-slavery Bugle* that defended the actions of those who freed Salem. The brochure recommends finishing a tour of these places (most of which are private homes) by visiting Freedom Hall, which is part of the Salem Historical Society Museum.

5

CUYAHOGA COUNTY

The Sly-Fanner Murders

In 1920, on New Year's Eve, Wilfred C. Sly, the owner of the W.W. Sly Manufacturing Company, and his company's superintendent, George J. Fanner, got into a car with the between $4,200 and $4,500 worth of payroll withdrawn from a bank. While returning to the factory, which Sly's father had been established in 1875 to make equipment for foundries, their car crossed over Nickle Plate Bridge on West Seventeenth Street. Then—*bam*! Another vehicle crashed into theirs, forcing them off the road and causing their vehicle to flip onto its side.

This occurred in the Cleveland neighborhood of Old Brooklyn, whose borders span east to west from the Cuyahoga River to the city of Brooklyn (no relation to the neighborhood) and south to north from Parma to Brookside Park. The current neighborhood traces its origin back to the village of Brighton. Carved out of land from a farm that belonged Warren Young, the village's first attempt at becoming an incorporated municipality was short-lived. In 1836, Samuel H. Barstow secured the village's incorporation, and the next year, he secured its mayorship. Less than a year later, the village's citizens decided to allow the village charter to expire. In 1889, the village reincorporated as South Brooklyn. The village of South Brooklyn ceased to exist on December 11, 1905, when the Cleveland City Council voted to annex it. This was a mutual decision, the village council having voted in favor of it on December 2, 1903.

Eyewitness and newspaper accounts vary on some of the details about what happened after the collision on the Nickle Plate Bridge, although they all agree on the basic points. Sly and Fanner were gunned down in cold blood by a band of five robbers. According to one report, Mrs. Maude Toohey saw the incident and inserted herself into it, as she knew Sly. She asked him if he was alright. As she did so, the bandit who was driving the car that hit Sly's started telling him that it was his fault.

A bandit grabbed the money bag while another drew his revolver and shot Sly in the heart. One account reported that Sly was shot once in the stomach and twice in the head, making quite the mess of his face; another said that the bandits had demanded the payroll and that Sly was only shot when he attempted to draw out his revolver. The man who killed Sly then shot Fanner—or, possibly, Fanner wrestled the money bag back and made a run for it but was gunned down by the three robbers. The robbers piled into a second car and took off, leaving Mrs. Toohey unharmed. That the bandits didn't kill or kidnap her makes sense. The event occurred around 11:00 a.m. and was witnessed by about twenty people, so the bandits could hardly have killed the whole lot of them to prevent later identification.

The car that crashed into Fanner and Sly had been stolen and belonged to the president of the Cleveland Trust Company, Fred H. Goff. His vehicle had been made by the F.B. Stearns Company, one of the many auto manufacturers in Cleveland at a time when it rivaled Detroit for the diversity of its a car production. The company's cars were known for their quality and luxury. The bandits had chosen this heavy vehicle because it was perfect for ramming another car.

Compared to other automakers, F.B. Stearns produced only a few cars a year. In 1903, it made eighty. It eventually had Albert Kahn, the man who designed Henry Ford's Highland Park and River Rouge Factories, build a factory that would be able to mass produce cars, but even then, it only made three thousand cars in 1916 and four thousand the next year. In 1925, the company was sold to John H. Willys, whose company Willys-Overland later made the first civilian Jeep. Stearns was one of the Great Depression's earliest casualties. It shuttered on December 20, 1929.

The bandits' getaway car was made by the Jordon Motor Car Company, another Cleveland manufacturer. Established in 1916 by Edward "Ned" S. Jordon, it didn't actually design its own cars; rather, it cobbled them together using existing parts from a variety of suppliers, making these Frankenstein's monsters at a low cost and therefore competitive with Ford Motor's Model T. Although Ford started offering the Model T in colors other than black in 1913, it never came close to the variety offered by Jordon, which produced cars painted in three different reds, two greens, two blues, two grays and one bronze.

Cleveland's F.B. Stearns Factory was located on Euclid and Lake Avenues. *Courtesy of the Library of Congress.*

One eyewitness of the Sly-Fanner murders wrote down part of the escaping Jordon's license plate number, which the bandits hadn't bothered to cover up. Within twenty-four hours of the murders, Inspector Charles N. Sterling used the information to locate the vehicle in the Hotel Winton's Bolivar Road garage. This led to the arrest of Dominick Benigno, Angelo Amato and Dominic Lonardo. Despite a staggeringly high bail of $70,000 each—far more than what had been stolen—they all made bail within an hour. Inspector Sterling had bagged the right men, but a grand jury declined to indict them. Despite this early arrest, days after the murders, associates and friends of Sly and Fanner posted a reward of $5,000 for the murderers' apprehension and conviction.

The case broke with the arrest of seventeen-year-old Ignatius "Sam" Purpera in Los Angeles on March 11, 1921. Although his parents were from Sicily, Purpera had been born in Cleveland and, after leaving school around the age of fourteen or fifteen to become a barber, had gotten into a life of petty crime. He had first come to the attention of Cleveland's police when they arrested him for stealing a car. Thrown into the boy's detention home, the over six-foot-tall boy escaped on December 13, 1920, and then made his way to Pittsburgh, where federal authorities arrested him. Given bail, he jumped it and headed back to Cleveland.

After the robbery, Purpera traveled to Boston, Philadelphia, Chicago, El Paso and Juarez, Mexico, which he entered and left using forged passports. He then made his way to San Francisco, where he stole a car for a drive to Los Angeles. Along the way, one of the car's bearings burned out, forcing him to stop for repairs in San Miguel at a garage run by C.J. Larsen. Larsen became suspicious of Purpera, who was calling himself George Palmer. Larsen reported him to Henry J. Raymond of the Southern California Automotive Association. Los Angeles police arrested Purpera upon his arrival in the city, and for reasons that were never made clear, the bandit confessed to his participation in the Cleveland crime. Being only seventeen years old, he believed he was exempt from the death penalty.

At first, Purpera refused to give up the names of his fellow bandits, though he later changed his mind about that. His version of the story differed from the eyewitness accounts. He claimed there were six men involved, though there were only five. He said he had been driving the Stearns and that after he got out, he started apologizing profusely for what he'd done. Then the Jordon pulled up and out came the other four to rob and ultimately murder Fanner and Sly. It was when Sly pointed his gun at Purpera that the others opened fire on the factory owner. Purpera never admitted to shooting anyone. After their getaway, the bandits split, and Purpera never saw a penny from the crime. While he was still in Cleveland, a detective who knew him by sight walked into the restaurant, forcing him to escape out the back.

Purpera was not the mastermind behind the robbery. The man who planned it was Louis Komer, known as the Toledo Kid. He had noticed that Sly and Fanner went to the bank around the same time every Friday and that they used the same route to ferry the cash back to their factory. One day, while in a pool hall, Komer heard Frank Motto from the Serra Gang complain that he was due to go to prison because he'd been convicted for stealing three cars. He said that if he had $1,500 to pay for an appeal, he might have his lengthy sentence reduced. Komer said he knew where to get that money, and a heist was planned. Benigno, Lonardo and Amato, associates of the Mayfield Road Mob, were brought in as gunmen. Benigno recruited Purpera the night before the robbery to help obtain the needed cars. The latter got the Stearns from Clarence Brown, the man who had stolen it from Goff.

With Purpera available to identify his compatriots, Cleveland police could arrest the others. Detective Charles Cavolo learned that Benigno and another suspect, Charles Colletti, were in Mexico. The cash-strapped and notoriously corrupt Cleveland Police Department had no money to send anyone to retrieve the fugitives, so Fred Caley from the Cleveland Automobile Club offered to pay the bill. Cavolo and Detective George Matowitz went to Mexico City under the guise of being agents of the auto club. There they visited with the American consul with plans to head to Guadalajara.

In one of those little coincidences that seem only to appear in fiction, right after leaving the meeting, they came across Benigno and Colletti on the street. They immediately grabbed the fugitives but nearly got lynched when Benigno riled up the crowd in Spanish, a language neither detective spoke. Mexican police helped the two Americans get their quarry to a local jail, and extradition procedures began. The Mexican government dragged the process out for six weeks to retaliate against the United States' refusal to recognize Mexico's president Álvaro Obregón as legitimate. Finally, Obregón ordered the prisoners to be ejected from his country, but they were to be placed onto a ship bound for Spain in Vera Cruz; from there, extradition proceedings would have to begin again. After another month, the frustrated detectives smuggled their prisoners onto the American ship *Monterey* that was bound for New York. After reaching New York, the detectives put the prisoners into a Brooklyn jail.

Colletti was released for lack of evidence. Benigno went to Cleveland, where it took three trials to convict him. In the first, a juror became ill. The second resulted in a hung jury. Found guilty by the third, Benigno was sentenced to death. He argued that he'd been framed and that Purpera had lied at the trial—but to no avail. He was executed on June 14, 1922. Purpera, to his surprise and horror, was also sentenced to die, and the State of Ohio duly executed him.

In January 1921, Frank Motto voluntarily showed up at the Mansfield Reformatory to serve his sentence for car theft, his ill-gotten money having done him no good in reducing his sentence. After details of the crime came to light, Motto was charged with murder. Nine days later, Louis Komer was arrested in Detroit. He, too, confessed, even going so far as to lead police to two of the guns used in the crime. Like the rest of the robbers, he claimed he never fired a shot. For his part, Komer received a life sentence. Motto, when found guilty, was sentenced to death by a female judge, the first time this ever occurred in Ohio. It was also notable that the foreman of the jury, Edith Markell, was also a woman.

Angelo Amato evaded capture for many years. Although authorities knew he'd gone to Italy, they lost his trail. It was not until he returned to America to attend a funeral in 1934 that he was he finally arrested. Being an Italian citizen, he was tried in Italy, where members of the Cleveland Police Department went to testify. He was found guilty on April 11, 1935.

6

ERIE COUNTY

The Confederate Plot to Liberate Johnson Island's Civil War POW Camp

S oon after the outbreak of the Civil War, a place for prisoners of war was erected near Sandusky on Johnson's Island. Today, nothing remains of the original camp. Some artifacts can be found in the Follet House Museum in Sandusky. Johnson's Island was originally called Bull's Island, named after E.W. Bull, who tried and failed to establish a town there. Its name changed when it came into the possession of Leonard Johnson. During the Civil War, the government rented the island from him for $500 a year.

The plan was to accommodate 1,000 prisoners. It soon became apparent that the war would last far longer than expected, meaning there were going to be many more POWs. So, it was decided to expand the camp's capacity to 2,800. Built on the southeastern part of the island, which Johnson had already cleared, prisoners started arriving on April 10, 1862. Secretary of War Edwin M. Stanton determined that the camp would only hold officers, although some enlisted men were kept there. When the Union stopped prisoner exchanges with the Confederacy at the end of 1864, the camp's population spiked to over 3,000.

The camp had twelve barracks surrounded by a twelve-foot-high fence that was guarded by sentinels on a parapet. Inside, the prisoners slept in three-tiered bunks with tick-infested straw mattresses and a single blanket for each man. During the winter, the intense cold made them miserable, a situation that was worsened after 9:00 p.m., when all fires and lights had to be extinguished. Decent clothing was not to be had, save for what outsiders

This letter was written on Johnson's Island by POW J.F. [Moon?] to Doctor George Brown. It is dated February 23, 1865. *Courtesy of the Library of Congress.*

sent the prisoners. Prisoners diverted themselves with music, baseball and a debating club.

Since they were officers, most prisoners came from the southern aristocracy, meaning that they had access to money to make their stays a bit more pleasant. One inmate, Captain Ezekiel John Ellis, recorded in his diary that he disliked washing day because it was his day to cook, so he solved this problem by hiring someone to do his washing for him. His money couldn't, however, make a cooked cat more appetizing. He intended to give it a try, but in the end, he couldn't bring himself to eat it.

When Colonel Ben Johnson, who had led the Fifteenth Arkansas Infantry, arrived in the fall of 1863, he didn't consider the prison overcrowded, thought the rations were good and found the sutler's store—a sutler sold men of the army provisions—well stocked. From the store, one could buy nearly anything—except for liquor. For his first winter, Johnson received two blankets for warmth, which were poorly made, hairy and certainly had no contributions from sheep. He received no other blankets for the rest of the war. He quipped that the mattresses barely had enough straw in them to make a meal for a cow. (He had possibly never lived on a farm, as cows eat hay). In the summer of 1864, the sutler departed, and rations diminished considerably. That fall, the prisoners were given a new half ration, something called whitefish that was probably carp and not especially palatable. Soon, the camp's previously robust rat population mysteriously disappeared.

The camp's first commandant, William Pierson, was removed in January 1864 for abusing prisoners. Smallpox broke out in block no. 13 in the winter of 1864–65. Only ten to twelve men were afflicted, and of those men, two or three died. The latter were buried in the cemetery that was laid out on the northern part of the island. According to the National Park Service's website, there are 206 gravestones still standing, and thanks to ground-penetrating radar, 267 men were found to have been buried there. For many years, the Daughters of the Confederacy took care of the cemetery, but they donated one acre of the land to the federal government in 1931.

These POWs had not been forgotten by their brethren in the Confederate army. A plot to rescue them was conceived by John Yates Beall, a Virginian who had been born on January 1, 1835. Beall's father, George, owned a farm called Walnut Groove, which Beall took over in 1855. When the war broke out, Beall joined as an officer in the Stonewall Brigade. Seriously wounded in 1861, he rejoined in 1862 and participated in the 1862 Shenandoah Valley Campaign, during which he got cut off from his unit. Unable to reconnect, he headed to Iowa, where his brother gave him a job. In danger of being outed as a Confederate, he fled to Canada.

In January 1863, Beall went to Richmond. There, with the help of another former Stonewall Brigade officer, Colonel Edwin Gray Lee, he met with Jefferson Davis and proposed two plans. The first was to rescue prisoners from Johnson's Island, with the idea of marching them to Columbus to free

This photograph, taken by Samuel Anderson between 1861 and 1863, is of Johnson Island POW Lieutenant John Summerfield Lanier of Company K, Fourteenth Mississippi Infantry Regiment, Confederate army. *Courtesy of the Library of Congress.*

even more POWs at Camp Chase. The combined force would then wreak havoc across Ohio, forcing the Union to send more troops into the state, which would, in turn, give the Confederates the advantage they needed to defeat the Union army. It was more delusion than a workable plan.

Jefferson must have realized that, as he went with Beall's second proposal instead, which was to send a guerrilla naval raider into Chesapeake Bay. Beall became an acting master in the Confederate navy, with Colonel Lee as captain. After Lee's departure, Beall took command and wrought all sorts of havoc until he and his men were finally captured. After being released in a prisoner exchange, Beall made his way to Canada; from there, he planned to execute his plan to rescue POWs from Johnson's Island.

In the early weeks of August 1864, Charles H. Cole checked into Sandusky's West House Hotel on Columbus Avenue and Water Street. He asked one of the hotel's proprietors to hold several hundred dollars' worth of gold for him. Cole claimed to be a wealthy man from Philadelphia whose father owned several Pennsylvania coal mines. He had come to Sandusky to purchase two schooners that he planned to have sailed from the Great Lakes to the Atlantic via the St. Lawrence River; in the Atlantic, the vessels would be used to haul coal along the coast. Another account says he claimed to represent the Mount Hope Oil Company of Pennsylvania. It is probable that he spun more than one cover story. Cole tried to keep up the illusion of being in Sandusky on business by constantly receiving "updates" on stock shares and trade in cattle that were really coded reports.

A photograph of John Yates Beall from *President Lincoln and the Case of John Y. Beall*, by Isaac Markens. *Courtesy of Wikimedia Commons.*

It was hardly unusual that a wealthy person chose to stay at West House. Five stories tall, it was probably the largest hotel between Toledo and Cleveland. It had been started by brothers William T. and Abel Kingsbury West in 1858. William had arrived in Sandusky first—and not willingly. The story goes that while in Buffalo, New York, on his quest to find work during the Panic of 1837, his baggage was mistakenly put onto the wrong Lake Erie boat. Not wanting to be separated from it, he swam after it, but once on board, the captain refused to turn around and insisted on sailing to his destination of Sandusky. William's first business in town was a general store. Later, he and his brother decided to get into the hotel business to cater to the visitors of the 1858 Ohio State Fair that was being held in the city.

Representative Clement Vallandigham was the leader of the Ohio Copperheads. *Courtesy of the Library of Congress.*

Aside from making his business interests known, Cole began approaching Sandusky's Copperheads, northerners who sided with the southern cause. He frequented the house of outspoken Copperhead John H. Williams, who had taken in as guests two women who were the wives of POWs on Johnson's Island. A woman who did sewing for the Williamses heard Cole speak treasonous words. Cole also made friends with many of the officers on board the Union gunboat *Michigan*, often plying them with dinners and wine.

Two weeks after Cole's arrival, a southern refugee living in the city recognized him. He went to the authorities to inform them Cole was a Confederate officer. On Sunday, September 18, the *Michigan*'s skipper, Commander John C. Carter, sent Ensign C.C. Eddy to sleep at the West House to keep tabs on Cole, who was already under surveillance. Carter had received intelligence from Lieutenant Colonel Hill in Detroit that there was a plot to seize the *Michigan*, to which Carter replied that he was ready for it.

Cole invited all the boat's officers to a large supper on the night of September 20 that also included several prominent Copperheads from Sandusky. His invitation was accepted. On the afternoon of the gathering, Carter sent Ensign James Hunter to apprehend Cole. James brought Cole to the *Michigan*, where he was arrested. Cole quickly confessed that one of his Copperhead coconspirators, Dr. D.E. Stanley, was going to drug them all. Once incapacitated, Cole and local Copperheads Williams, John M. Brown, Captain Abraham Strain and F. Rosenthal planned to seize the *Michigan* and send a signal from it to let a Confederate raiding party know that the attack was on. The *Michigan* would then participate in Johnson's Island's rescue. Instead, Cole and his coconspirators spent the rest of the war on the island as its guests. Officials went through Cole's papers and discovered that he'd been paroled, meaning he was not supposed to fight against the Union in any way. For his part in this plot, he was imprisoned for the duration of the war.

The aforementioned Confederate raiding party had no idea that Cole had been compromised. Their part began on the morning of September 20, when Confederate agents boarded the sidewheel steamer *Philo Parsons*. The steamer had departed from Detroit with forty passengers on board. One of them approached the boat's clerk, W.O. Ashley, and informed him that four men in Old Sandwich Town, which is next to Windsor on the northern side of the Detroit River, also wished to board. Ashley informed Captain S.F. Atwood, so he ordered the *Parsons* to sail there. The men who boarded included Beall. The *Parsons* stopped at several more Canadian ports, and at Amherstburg, a trunk was brought on board.

Although the *Parsons*'s final destination was Sandusky, it first stopped at North Bass Island to drop Captain Atwood off at his home. Afterward, it steamed to Kelleys Island. As it left the dock, four men with revolvers entered Ashley's office and seized him. Led by Beall and his lieutenant, Bennet G.

Burley, the Confederates took from the chest that was brought on board in Amherstburg navy revolvers, hatchets, a grappling hook and a Confederate flag. Sources vary on how many Confederates were involved, but it was likely twenty. These pirates—for such is anyone who seizes a vessel on a body of water—met no resistance from the other passengers, who were put into the hold along with those seamen who were not needed.

Another lake steamer, the screw propeller–driven *Island Queen*, had departed from Sandusky around 3:00 p.m. that afternoon and went to Kelleys Island to pick up about thirty or forty men who had recently been mustered out of the Union army in Toledo. It then headed to Middle Bass Island, where it pulled up beside the *Parsons*. The Rebels boarded the *Island Queen*, informing its commander, Captain Orr, that he and his passengers were their prisoners. Disinclined to take on this role, some of the crew and passengers fought back. Shots were fired. The Rebels struck the *Island Queen*'s fireman on the head and seriously wounded passenger Lorenzo Miller from Put-in-Bay. The engineer was shot through the cheek for refusing to come out of the engine room.

Captain Orr and his officers were kept on board the *Parsons*, while the passengers from both vessels were put to shore and told not to raise the alarm. The *Parsons* towed the *Island Queen* south of Pelee Island, and there, an engine feed pipe was opened to scuttle the vessel. It settled onto the Chickenolee Reef at a depth of about seven feet, allowing it to be raised and put back into service a couple of days later.

The Rebels sailed the *Parsons* into Sandusky Bay and waited for Cole's rocket signal from Sandusky. Three hours passed. Unnerved that the signal had not come, seventeen of the twenty Rebels on board mutinied, refusing to go any closer to land for fear of having been discovered. Beall made them sign a paper attesting that this is what they had done. They made for Canada at top speed, dropping off Captain Orr and the other captives on Canada's Fighting Island in the Detroit River along the way. The Confederates tried to burn the *Parsons* at Old Sandwich Town but were prevented from doing so. Then they scattered. The *Parsons* was towed to Detroit. The next morning, the *Michigan* sailed to Kelleys Island, where its crew learned the fate of the *Parsons* and *Island Queen*—so ended the ill-fated raid on Johnson's Island.

Burley made his way back into the United States and rejoined the Confederate navy, where he became an acting master. After being severely wounded and captured, he was thrown into Fort Delaware, from which he, along with several other prisoners, escaped by climbing through a sewer pipe into the Delaware River. Picked up by a vessel heading to Philadelphia, he continued north into New York State and finally to Toronto, Canada, where he came across Beall. Burley drew the attention of authorities when he started experimenting with ordnance. When arrested, authorities initially mistook him for Beall, giving the latter time to escape the city.

Beall joined a small band of Rebels who planned to derail trains in order to rescue Confederate prisoners. On December 16, 1864, he was captured in Niagara Falls, New York. Briefly jailed in New York City, he was taken to Fort Layfette on January 5, 1865, to be tried for his roles in the failed Johnson's Island raid and in the train sabotage plot. His defense lawyer, James T. Brady, argued that Beall was just following orders as a Confederate naval officer, but this failed to convince anyone. Convicted, he was taken to Fort Columbus on Governors Island in New York Harbor and hanged on February 25, 1865.

7

GEAUGA COUNTY

The Village of Burton

The first people of European descent to settle in what would become the village of Burton were Tom and Lydia Umberfield and their five children (with four more to come after settling in Ohio). They had come from Connecticut and acquired their land through the Connecticut Land Company, which owned the Western Reserve. The Umberfield family brought with them oxen, horses, sheep, a cow, chickens and possibly the first domestic cats to come to Ohio. The felines were kept in the wagon to catch any mice that were trying to eat the supply of flour and sugar. The family possessed a quantity of sand because they didn't think it was available in Ohio. They took two months just to reach Fairport Harbor.

Traveling from Connecticut to Ohio by wagon was no easy task. One early settler family who arrived in 1815 used a one-horse wagon that took thirty-six days to go from Connecticut to Nelson, Ohio, in Portage County. By the time they arrived, Natives no longer posed a danger in the area through which they traveled—but bears and wolves did. One never went out at night without a torch for fear of encountering one or the other. One winter night, wolves came and scared their sheep so badly that eight of them jumped out of their pen; they were found dead in the morning.

Living in a cabin was challenging for settlers of the Western Reserve. In one family's split-log-floor cabin, the children didn't sit to eat at the crude table; rather, they ate standing up. Food was eaten in shifts in order of sex and age. First came the father, then the oldest son, and after the last of the males ate, the oldest girl went. The last to eat was the mother. When guests came, the meat was placed in the center of the table, and everyone who wanted some food used their knife and fork to get it. The family had few dishes at first and were ecstatic when a trader named Luke Vokes from Trumbull County arrived, peddling wooden dishes. The trouble with this sort of dishware was that it wore out quickly. The first nonwooden dishes the family possessed were made from yellow clay.

The Umberfields arrived at their new plot of land, lot 35, on June 21, 1798. After two months of clearing a spot—the old-growth trees there were huge, some more than four feet wide—Tom built a cabin that initially lacked a floor, windows and even a door (the entrance was covered with stretched deerskin). Natives taught the family the three sisters planting scheme. First, you plant corn, then beans that wrap themselves around the cornstalks and, finally, you sow something to cover the rest of the ground, like pumpkins, squash or cucumbers. The Natives also taught the family how to dry corn, which they made popcorn with, eaten plain.

All nine of the Umberfield children survived to adulthood, an unusual occurrence in an age with high child mortality rates. One of the Umberfield girls, Stella, married into the prominent Hickox family. By the time her father reached his nineties, he had gone blind. Concerned for his welfare, Stella tried to get him to move in with her, but he refused to leave his house. Undaunted, she had his home moved besides hers. Though this is no longer the case, at the time, the two residences were connected. Tom Umberfield died in 1850, a year after the death of his wife, at the ripe old age of ninety-six.

This was no more unusual then than it is today and would've stunned no one. But when one hears that the average human lifespan was thirty-six in this era, it conjures up an image of a world bereft of the elderly. Average age is one of the most useless statistics historians can report, as it tells you absolutely nothing. Real human lifespan has not changed in two thousand years. The reason the average age has increased so dramatically in the last few centuries isn't because people are living longer; rather, it is due to the massive decrease in infant and child mortality rates. If 12 percent of all infants and children die, the average age will skew far lower than reality warrants. So, if you hopped into a time machine and visited London in 1500 CE, you would see plenty of old people who had made it into their seventies, eighties and even a few into their nineties.

Another early settler in Burton was Peter Hitchcock. Born on October 18, 1781, in Cheshire, Connecticut, he graduated from Yale in 1801 and was admitted to the Connecticut Bar Association in 1804. Marrying Nabby

Interior of the Hickox House, Century Village Museum. *Photograph taken by the author.*

Cook in 1805, the next year, the newlyweds moved to Burton, where they welcomed their first child, Reuben, on September 2. At the outbreak of the War of 1812, Hitchcock joined the army as an adjunct officer. In 1814, he joined the Fourth Regiment of the Ohio State Militia as a lieutenant colonel.

After the war, Hitchcock returned to Burton to practice law. He also got into politics and became a Whig politician and judge at the state level, eventually becoming the chief justice of the Ohio Supreme Court. He helped with the 1851 revisions to Ohio's constitution. Heavily involved in Burton's Congregational church, Hitchcock died peacefully in 1854 with his last words being, "Oh, my children, all be Christians." His house is currently located in Century Village. Built in 1824, it was originally located a mile north of the village and housed Hitchcock's descendants until 1884.

Early settlers were quick to take advantage of Geauga County's natural resources, including maple syrup. The first European record of maple syrup's existence was made by French explorer André Thevet in 1557, but no one knows how long America's indigenous people had been making maple syrup before he saw it. By 1885, Geauga County was the largest maple syrup producer in the United States.

This trunk slice, which came from a maple tree in Burton, shows the many taps that were put into it during its life, Century Village Museum. *Photograph taken by the author.*

In Geauga County, the sugaring season (as it is known) usually spanned from mid-February to April. Trees were tapped with a metal spout that emptied the sap into a bucket. The sap was put into galvanized iron gathering tanks and hauled to sugarhouses, where it was poured into storage vats from which it was fed by a pipe into an evaporator. From here, the sap was strained. Most of the sap was made into syrup, but some of it was made into sugar. To make the latter, the sap was placed into sugar pans, boiled to a specific temperature, then left to cool. The cakes usually weighed between one and one and a half pounds. To make syrup, the strained sap was allowed to cool, then reheated and cooled once more. At the end of each sugaring season, friends and families gathered for a sugaring-off party. At these parties, a favorite food was sugar-on-snow, which is produced by heating maple syrup to 235 degrees Fahrenheit, then drizzling it over packed snow. It was often served on a wooden spoon or wooden stick, though some people ate it with their hands.

In 1893, Burton resident Albert Joseph Thrasher thought it might be a good idea to promote Geauga County's maple products at the upcoming World's Columbian Exposition in Chicago, which, among other firsts, was where the Ferris wheel debuted, powered by the newfangled source of power known as electricity. Other maple producers agreed that having a presence at the fair would be a good idea, so Thrasher presented the idea to Ohio's governor William McKinley, who got the Ohio General Assembly to fund it. Thrasher became the project's superintendent. He employed the Cleveland architectural firm Lehman & Schmidt to design the exhibit and then paid the West Side Furniture Company to build it. The Geauga County maple exhibit appeared in the fair's agricultural building.

8

HARRISON COUNTY

The Ohio Coal Industry

I t's easy to forget that thirty of Ohio's eighty-eight counties contain a massive reserve of coal, which was once mined in twenty-two counties and was part of the state's industrial might before it became an unwilling member of the Rust Belt. About twelve thousand square miles of Ohio's soil have coal buried underneath, most of it in the state's southern and eastern regions. At one point in Ohio's history, coal generated over $1 billion a year. The state's coal seams are just part of those that spread throughout Appalachia.

Harrison County benefited greatly from its coal reserves. Formed in 1813, the county was named for William Henry Harrison, the man known for massacring Natives and being America's first president to die in office, just thirty-two days after taking his oath of office. Cadiz became the county seat. Bypassed by canals and the new National Road, Harrison County was largely isolated from major trade routes until the arrival of the railroads in the mid-1850s. Coal mining in the county started in the 1830s but didn't became a major contributor to the county's economy until the latter part of the 1930s. Until then, most people in the area were farmers.

Farming has always consisted of long days, hard work and constant anxiety over what the weather might bring, but coal miners had it far worse. In early coal mines, standing up was not an option; miners were forced to crawl and crouch. Years of breathing in coal dust often led to black lung, though whether a miner lived long enough to suffer from this ailment was a crapshoot.

Coal mines were—and, to a degree, still are—filled with all sorts of life-threatening risks. There were explosive gases and coal dust, made all the more dangerous in the days when miners used open flames for illumination. Poisonous gases also posed a hazard, so miners brought with them birds—usually canaries—and if the birds stopped singing, miners knew to immediately evacuate the area. Safety equipment was slowly introduced to counteract these hazards, but even today, major mining disasters still occur in the United States.

In 1936, Eleanor Roosevelt visited the Hanna Coal Company's Willow Grove Coal Mine, near Bellaire in Belmont County. At noon on March 16, 1940, a speeding mine car burst out of its entrance, carrying an unconscious driver. It was the first indication that something terrible had happened below. An explosion, followed by a fire, swept through the shafts. According to one newspaper account, of the 157 miners who were working that day, 72 escaped into an airshaft at the end of a drift, but it did them little good. They all died. Mine superintendent John Richards and tipple boss Howard Sanders tried to organize a rescue, but they were both were killed by black damp, which is air consisting of mostly carbon dioxide and nitrogen.

Inspectors of the damage turned back when poisonous air killed two of their canaries. Rescuers who were wearing masks attached to forty-pound oxygen tanks found that the destruction was far worse than expected. The body of one man was twisted unnaturally against the mine car that had crushed him. Braces were shattered. A mine train consisting of twenty steel cars pulled by a sixteen-ton engine had been demolished, the engine thrown 150 feet from where it had originally been.

Each victim's family received $5,250 in compensation. Dependents were also eligible for Social Security. But this money, however generous, couldn't bring back dead loved ones. William Brown, a machine operator, believed the catastrophe could have been prevented. The company knew explosive gas was present, as its presence had caused three minor explosions nine months earlier.

A company engineer, John Hartley, insisted that no gas had been present at that time. Indeed, Willow Grove had been officially designated as gas free. But any mine that went as deep as this one was going to hit pockets of gas. This didn't mean an explosion was inevitable. Proper ventilation could have cleared the gas out. Regularly sweeping out dangerous coal dust or wetting it and covering it with crushed rock could have prevented it from becoming dangerous. Willow Grove implemented none of these safety measures because it deemed the cost too high.

This 1908 photograph, taken at Brown Mine in Brown, West Virginia, shows a good example of a child mine worker. *Courtesy of the Library of Congress.*

The explosion was likely caused by something miners call "windy shot." This is when the thickness of the seam is overestimated and too much explosive is used. When detonated, the resulting explosion pushes smoke and flame back into the open shaft. Miners take precautions to avoid being engulfed by this, but if the flames find flammable gas or excessive coal dust, it can cause an explosion.

As if the dangers of working in a coal mine were not enough, miners were economically exploited by their employers. Until unionization put a stop to it, miners had traditionally been paid by the carload, not the hour. To increase their output, some miners brought in their wives on the sly. Their children, too, were put to work. Ida Mae Stull, in Scio, Ohio, began carrying her father's lantern when she was six or seven years old.

Stull didn't know the exact year she'd been born, but she did know her birthday was on February 2. In an interview she gave in 1976, she believed herself to be over eighty years old, meaning she was born before 1896. One of eighteen children, she never learned to read or write. She attended a school in Smithfield, Ohio, but was expelled for beating up the other kids who tormented her for being different. Born with a crooked leg, at the time, she was made to wear heavy shoes and iron braces. She grew to a height of five feet and seven inches and had two daughters, both of whom were struck by a trolley in Bellaire; only one of them, Mary, survived. Stull became a full-time coal miner because her husband, Marion Hennis, refused to work. Once, she caught him napping in a haystack, so she set his shoes on fire while they were still on his feet.

By 1934, Stull was earning two dollars a day in the Megan Mine, which was located near Cadiz. When mine inspector Andrew Mullen caught her working in the mine, he reported her presence because Ohio state law forbade women from working in hazardous occupations, including mining. John Berry, the head of the Division of Ohio Mines, came in person to remove her. For his trouble, she pelted him with rotten eggs. No one had paid much attention to her until Mullen arrived.

A lawyer from Cadiz, John G. Worley, got the decision to remove her from the mine reversed in 1935—so, back to work she went. Newsreel cameras were there to record her work. Some considered her the first woman to work in a coal mine, but it seems more likely that women had been working under the radar in mines for a long time before she was caught. She claimed she could fill six or seven cars a shift, a pace that would have killed a man. She eventually left the mine to start a dairy farm, which she continued to work on until 1966, when a bull that was chasing her caused her fall 150 feet over a strip mine wall. She died in 1980.

Many coal companies that were operating in Appalachia built their own towns for their workers. While this sounds altruistic, it was, in truth, insidious. In their early days, many mining towns were nothing more than camps, and those with frame houses weren't necessarily an improvement. In 1925, the U.S. Coal Commission reported that most dwellings lacked running water and plumbing. Privies often emptied into a nearby creek.

To pay for the construction of a town, a mining company forced its employees to rent their housing and forbade them from buying property elsewhere. The mine company had a private police force to keep the workers in line, especially if they got any ideas about unionization. In addition to rent, workers had deducted from their monthly pay the cost of utilities and, in some cases, school fees and taxes. If a miner died, his family was evicted from their home, sometimes with just ten days' notice. If a miner was injured and couldn't work, his family found themselves homeless. Eviction was also a consequence suffered by those who dared to go on strike.

Workers were usually paid in scrip in lieu of money, and this scrip was virtually worthless outside of the company store. Outside peddlers and other

A mine car from the Abel Mine, Harrison County History of Coal Museum. *Photograph taken by the author.*

businesses were barred from entering the mining towns in order to maintain the stores' monopolies. When workers ran out money before the next paycheck—and they usually did—they could get credit from the company store, which was notorious for charging inflated prices. Historian Alex P. Schust argued that this was because workers who got credit would go work for another coal company and leave their bill unpaid, forcing the store to raise prices to compensate. Mines, Schust proposed, created company stores not out of greed but out of necessity. There just weren't any independent stores that were willing to set up shop by a mining community for fear that the mine would go bust.

Still another historian, John A. Enman, did a thorough study of company store prices. For this, he chose the Union Supply Company, a business established in 1898 that was a subsidiary of the H.C. Frick Coke Company. Looking at its account books for meat for 1905–6, he found that the prices there were about the same as they were independent stores. Stores that charged excessive prices tended to be inefficient or were not operated full time. While his data were likely correct, his conclusion may not be applicable to small or independent company stores. He had, after all, examined the books of a chain.

Some former miners and their family members had fond memories of the company store. There, people gathered on their days off to socialize. The stores sold groceries, clothes, furniture, toys, appliances and mining equipment (the company certainly wasn't going to provide that) and had a butcher. At the soda fountain, a person could get ice cream. The stores offered access to a telegraph and telephone. You could even pay your bills there. If the store didn't have what you wanted, you could order it through a catalog. You didn't even do the shopping; a clerk got everything you wanted.

Terrible working conditions and constant impoverishment prompted miners to form unions, the most powerful and well known of which was the United Mine Workers of America (UMWA). It formed in Columbus, Ohio, in 1908, when the National Progressive Miners Union and Knights of Labor Assembly 135 combined. It was initially composed of British and American pick miners. In 1897, the union fronted a 100,000-man strike that resulted in the Central Competitive Field Agreement the next year, giving miners higher wages and union recognition in five Midwestern states. The UMWA soon expanded into Pennsylvania, where its membership was much more ethnically diverse. It lost much of its gains in the 1920s and first years of the 1930s until the passage of the National Industrial Recovery Act in June 1933 gave legal protections for unionization.

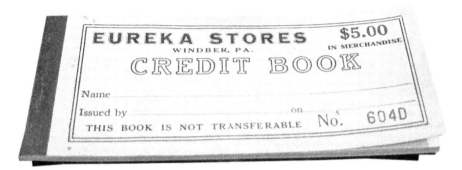

An example of scrip from the Eureka Company Store, Harrison County History of Coal Museum. *Photograph taken by the author.*

The coal industry had a profound effect on the world above the mines. While this book's author was on a rafting trip in West Virginia with a group, their guide, a former coal miner from a family who had been in the business for generations, told them that when the coke ovens that once burned high above the river on either side were in use, the entire area was covered in black dust. Coke is nearly pure carbon and used mostly in blast furnaces. The byproducts of coke and coal have been used many products that Americans will be familiar with, including insecticide, Denorex shampoo and conditioner (it contains coal tar), Monteil Galore cologne, the plastic in screwdrivers, golf balls and putty. Coal ash is also recycled into other materials, such as roofing shingles, grit for abrasives and concrete blocks.

9

HOLMES COUNTY

The Amish

T he Amish have never shaped Ohio's history in an overt way. Their quiet lives and isolation from the larger world are so profound that when the author went looking for historically significant Amish personages who helped to change the course of state history, he found none. This isn't to say that the Amish haven't had their own impact on history, especially in the regions where they live. Their very presence in Holmes County gives it a unique character. Certainly, the Amish contribution to the economy of Holmes County is significant. One can start with their many small businesses, especially their furniture-making businesses. This is a lucrative venture, as people associate quality workmanship with Amish-made goods, and the author of this book is not immune to this. The keyboard he used to type these words was set atop an Amish-made computer desk. Behind him is an Amish-made bookshelf. And in the author's dining room is an Amish-made table and chair set.

The Amish call outsiders to their community "English." Unlike most organized religions, the Amish have no church buildings. Instead, each community, which usually consists of twenty-five to forty families, meets at someone's house every other week for religious services that last for three hours; one of these hours is set aside for a cappella singing. Musical instruments and dancing are forbidden. Women wear their "good" clothes to these services. Most Amish dresses have aprons, a sign of modesty. Zippers are forbidden, so clothes are held together with straight pins, though some orders allow the use of safety pins. Married women wear black dresses with white aprons. Unmarried women don black caps.

The Amish, who do not drive automobiles, rely on horse-drawn buggies for transportation, Yoder's Amish Home. *Photograph taken by the author.*

At weddings, the brides wear blue dresses with white aprons. Like regular services, weddings are held at someone's home. Unlike their English counterparts, these affairs last all day, with guests being served two full meals. Beforehand, everyone prays, and no one leaves the table until the last person is done. The Amish don't have arranged marriages, though members of the church are forbidden from marrying the English. Amish are not required to marry, and some remain single all their lives.

The Amish are Anabaptists, meaning they believe in adult baptism. Young adults are given the choice to join the church. Those who do are considered full members upon being baptized. Once a year, those who wish to join the church declare themselves as candidates at a Sunday service, usually one held in the spring. After being taken to another room, they meet with the ministers to discuss what joining the church means and whether they're ready to commit. Those who are ready receive further instructions.

Each church has two ministers and a bishop. Anyone can be a minister. All who wish to be considered for the position are chosen by lot. The bishop is also chosen by lot, except this position comes from the pool of ministers. When they meet for Sunday services, ministers kiss one another on the lips. This "holy kiss" signifies peace and is derived from several passages found in the New Testament.

Amish Bibles are written in High German, which is also the language used in their formal prayers. Their everyday language is Pennsylvania Dutch (Dietsch), which was a language brought to America by the German Lutherans. Derived from High German, with many English words integrated into it, Pennsylvania Dutch is not the same as the Dutch spoken in the Netherlands. Amish tend to do most reading and writing in English, which is also used in their schools and when they interact with the English.

Church districts are governed by the *Ordnung* (order), the dictates of accepted behavior that are orally passed down to the members twice a year before communion. Although some matters are voted on, most of the time, the congregation follows its bishop's recommendations. Churches that share a similar *Ordnungs* are considered "in fellowship" and join an affiliation, allowing for the sharing of ministers and taking communion in another church if it is considered a full fellowship. There are twelve recognized Amish *Ordnungs*.

Holmes County has four affiliations that account for about 97 percent of the church districts there. The *Ordnungs* in Holmes County are the Swartzentrubers, Andy Weavers, Old Order and New Order. Of these, the Old Order Amish are the most numerous, and the Swartzentrubers are the most conservative. Unlike some of their less-conservative brethren, the Swartzentrubers have no windows in their buggies, no indoor plumbing and no linoleum floors. Men wear broad-brim hats, and women wear large bonnets. Men don't trim their beards. Most of them still farm and their homes have spartan interiors. They also don't observe Daylight Savings Time. But they're allowed to smoke tobacco, and they have an unexpected courtship practice called bundling.

Bundling works like this: a teenage boy and girl spend a night in the girl's bed together, fully clothed. The girl wears a nightdress called a *nacht rock* made of a fancy material that is a color not normally allowed, such as pink. No sexual contact is allowed. In times past, a wooden board was placed between the two. In some cases, the girl removes her outer dress or a knee-length one. Boys take off their shoes and sometimes their shirts. It is possible that this tradition, which traces its roots back to Europe, was either practiced because the couple needed to cuddle in an era of unheated rooms (not likely, considering the presence of board between them), or it was the only way the couple could have privacy, as Amish families tend to be large. Whatever its original purpose, it has caused quite a few schisms in the Amish community over the years.

Amish youth, after the age of sixteen, enter *Rumspringa*, or "running around," the time when they are given greater freedoms until their final commitment to join the church (which some choose not to). There is myth that this means these Amish youth are allowed to experience every sin they can manage before settling down to a more sedate life, but this isn't the case. Although some Amish teenagers do rebel and get into trouble that is not expected for someone of their upbringing, this is generally not the case.

These young people are allowed to visit friends and join activities without adult supervision. The more conservative Amish boys in Holmes County are allowed, for example, to take their buggy out on a Sunday night to go singing. In Lancaster County, Pennsylvania, the youth often join "gangs" of like-minded friends, and there, you might see Amish youth driving a car. Those who choose the path of baptism must give up forbidden things to church members, such as cell phones or cars. Children who die before reaching *Rumspringa* are believed to go straight to heaven.

Upon first arriving in America, the Amish were fairly uniform in their beliefs. They settled mainly in William Penn's colony of Pennsylvania because of its religious tolerance. The Amish were attacked during the French and Indian War and, thereafter, by other Protestant groups, such as the Baptists, Methodists and United Brethren. During the American Revolution, they tried to stay neutral, but neither the British nor Americans took kindly to that. By 1800, there were about one thousand Amish left in Pennsylvania, but between 1817 and 1860, about three thousand more came over from Europe.

The trouble was that these new Amish weren't nearly as conservative as the native lot, and religious schisms ensued. Out of this came the conservative Old Order Amish and the more reform-minded Amish Mennonites (separate from the mainstream Mennonites). More splintering ensued. There were the Elgy Amish, Stuckey Amish and the Sleeping Preaching Amish. Members of this last group fall asleep early in the evening, arise several hours later in an apparent trance and then preach about spiritual renewal, repentance and getting back a simple life.

Those Amish who settled in Holmes County in 1809 weren't immune to such divisions either. Holmes County's *Ordnungs* can trace their roots back to the Old Order Amish, who, despite the name, were less conservative than some of their offshoots. In the 1960s, for example, they decided to embrace Daylight Savings Time for the benefit of those who worked in factories. They are more likely to use cell phones and allow their unbaptized teenagers to own cars than their New Order counterparts. The New Order Amish allow their women to wear colorful clothes. Buggies can have rubber tires, telephones are allowed in the house and balloon tires can be used on farm equipment. They still refuse to connect to the electric grid, but they do have inverters and generators. Although they are not allowed to drive, they can ride in cars and fly in planes.

To understand all these schisms, one must go back to the dawn of the German Reformation and the rise of Anabaptism. Not baptizing infants was quite controversial. Traditional Christian dogma taught the necessity for this, else an infant or young child who died would not be allowed into heaven. Rebaptism was also not looked upon favorably. Authorities used a variety of methods to snuff out this heresy, including fines, imprisonment, confiscation of property, torture and death. Most of the movement's early leaders who participated in the first rebaptisms in 1525 lost their lives for their belief. Indeed, around 2,500 anabaptists were killed in the sixteenth and early seventeenth centuries, mostly in German speaking regions. Switzerland was the most zealous in stamping out Anabaptism.

One of the most influential Anabaptists was Menno Simmons, who was ordained as a Catholic priest in 1524. By the time he broke with the Catholic Church in 1536, he had a grim outlook on the world, which he believed was an inherently cruel place in which anabaptists could expect nothing less than persecution and death for their faith. As his first name suggests, he founded the Mennonites.

Around 1680, a tailor named Jakob Ammann, who had been born in 1644 and raised as a member of the Swiss Reformed Church, joined the Mennonites and became an elder. This gave him the power to baptize and oversee the blessing ceremony for communion. Sometime in the 1690s, he moved his family to the village of Sainte-Marie-aux-Mines in Alsace, a piece of land that both the Germans and French had claimed and controlled over the centuries. He was just one of many Mennonites there escaping Swiss persecution.

After settling in his new home, Ammann proposed new reforms that included increasing the number of times communion was presented from one to two times a year, the idea being that this would prompt Mennonites to consider their spiritual relationship with God more often. Like so many reformers who wanted a more conservative religion, Ammann felt that the Mennonites in his community weren't devout enough. He also proposed the idea of shunning, the ostracization of an individual from the community that varies in its severity but is a terrible blow to an Amish person.

Other elders strongly disagreed with Ammann, and in 1693, a heated debate among Swiss Mennonites erupted. During a scheduled day of meeting, seven ministers refused to come. This so enraged Ammann that he excommunicated the lot. And while he was at it, he excommunicated five ministers who had come to the meeting but hadn't sufficiently supported his position. Another meeting followed, but Ammann departed without listening to those who disagreed with him.

Ammann's followers broke off and started the Amish religion. The Mennonite communities in Switzerland soon shrunk to just three near the Alsatian border, no doubt in part because the Bern government urged and possibly forced the Mennonites and Amish to leave for North America. King Louis XIV of France expelled all of the Anabaptists from Alsace in 1712. Thereafter, Ammann's whereabouts are lost to history.

Ammann's dour outlook on the treatment of Anabaptists was doubtless motivated by the fact that many had been killed for their beliefs. It didn't take long for them to compare themselves to persecuted figures from the Old and New Testaments, such as Daniel, Moses, Jeremiah, Elijah, Jesus (who not only died on the cross but was tortured beforehand) and Paul, said to have been beheaded by Nero. The Amish associated moustaches with their persecutors, which explains why they decline to grow them.

It is amazing just how deeply the Amish conceive matters of theology, considering they all have nothing more than an eighth-grade education. This just shows that one doesn't need formal training to become well-learned in a subject. The reason the Amish object to high school education and beyond is because they believe it could lead to *hochmut*, or arrogance and pride. They also don't want their children exposed to the worldly curriculum they'd learn in high school.

In 1921, Ohio passed the Bing Act that compelled parents to send their children to school through the end of high school or until they reach the age of eighteen. Many Amish parents went to jail for refusing to comply. In Ohio, some local schoolboards made attempts to shut down the Amish-run schools themselves. In 1960, for example, the Hardin County Board of Education deemed these schools a "public nuisance" because Amish teachers lacked a college education. The counterargument pointed out that Amish preachers had no formal theological training, and no one complained about that. With the schools set to close, the Third Ohio District Court of Appeals ruled that the schoolboard couldn't close the schools. Other states were set to close their Amish schools, too, and when Wisconsin fined three Amish fathers five dollars for failing to enroll their children in high school, the case made its way to the U.S. Supreme Court. On May 15, 1972, the court ruled unanimously that the Amish were exempt from compulsory school after the eighth grade.

That the Amish are willing to suffer legal and other consequences for their convictions should come as no surprise, as they eschew so many modern things. They do this because they believe it is the way to be truly humble and live the way Jesus and the scriptures prescribed. Their nonconfrontational philosophy proscribes them from serving on juries, becoming police officers and holding political office. One source said it also prohibits them from filing lawsuits, and this may be true for some, but the author of this book found examples of several lawsuits brought forth by Amish individuals.

Sometimes, their reasoning for refusing to comply with the law on religious grounds is not clear. In June 1901, near Orville, Ohio, an Amish man named Daniel C. Liechty began using his farm to make phosphates from dead animals. Not surprisingly, neighbors objected to the smell, so a Green Township health officer came to inspect the operation. Deemed a nuisance, Liechty was arrested. When brought before the mayor of Orville for judgement, Liechty was fined one hundred dollars. Liechty refused to pay on the grounds of religious conviction, so he was instead sent to Stark County Infirmary, a workhouse where the poor were sent.

One of the core beliefs that Amish all follow is pacifism, even in cases of self-defense. The refusal of military service was too much for the European nations they came from. This belief challenged the power of the authorities and was one of the reasons Europeans persecuted the Amish. Until World War II, it was much the same in the United States. During World War I, some Amish draftees agreed to undergo training, but those who didn't suffered mental and physical abuse.

After the creation of the selective service on September 16, 1940, the secretary of the Joint Army-Navy Service Board Lewis Hershey asked representatives from the peace churches to propose alternative services. The latter were represented by the National Service Board for Religious Objectors. Its head, Paul French, suggested the government set up alternative service camps administered by the churches themselves. The camps would produce items that could cause no harm, such as clothing, food and medical care. In June 1941, some twenty camps were up and running. Although a

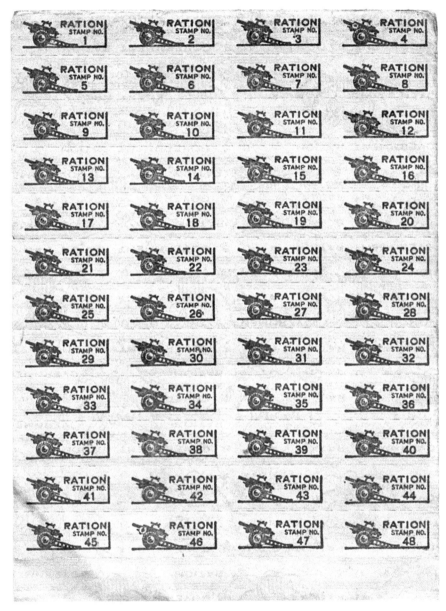

World War II ration book. The image of an artillery piece prompted many Amish to forgo using these stamps. *From the author's collection.*

few Amish chose to go to combat or take noncombative roles that assisted the military effort, most declared themselves conscientious objectors and went to the camps. Many Amish civilians wouldn't use the ration stamps issued by the government to prevent hoarding because there were military images on them. Although they were largely self-sufficient, they did without if the alternative meant using a stamp.

10

HURON COUNTY

The Fight to Color Margarine

Huron County is part of what was once known as the Firelands, itself a section of the Western Reserve. During the American Revolution, the British frequently raided Connecticut's coastal cities, often burning them. To compensate those affected, Connecticut set aside 500,000 acres at the western end of the Western Reserve, where victims could resettle. Huron and Erie are two of the counties that were carved from that area, as were parts of Ottawa and Ashland Counties. Some of the municipalities organized there were named for places that were attacked by the British, including New Haven, Fairfield and Norwalk. Beneficiaries sometimes sold their land to speculators instead of relocating to Ohio.

In the early days of settlement, most pioneers in the Firelands built log cabins. When a person or family set out to construct a cabin, it wasn't unusual for neighbors to travel from miles around to help. A person who was knowledgeable in building log cabins was chosen as head of the operation. Skilled axmen took to the task of carving notches into the logs so that they could be tightly interconnected. As in any construction area, accidents sometimes happened, their frequency increasing as the day progressed, thanks to the liberal imbibing of whiskey. At the end of the day, when the cabin was mostly finished and the men were sufficiently drunk, it wasn't unusual for a fight or two to break out.

Huron County's capital is Norwalk, and there, one can find the excellent Firelands Historical Society and Laning-Young Research Center. It consists of two buildings, the Laning-Young Research Center and the historic Wickham

House, which was built by Samuel Preston for his son-in law and daughter Frederick and Lucy Wickham, who were married in 1835. Frederick, a sailor on Lake Erie, arrived in the area via the Milan Canal. His father-in-law, Preston, had established what would become the *Norwalk Reflector* five years earlier, a paper that is still, as of this writing, being published six days a week. He used the house's upper floor to print his newspaper. Lucy convinced Frederick to abandon his life of boats to become the paper's editor, which he was for fifty years. Despite being the father of thirteen children, over the years, Frederick managed to find time to be the mayor of Norwalk, the president of the city's board of education, an associate judge on the Huron County Common Pleas Court and a state senator.

In the house's basement, one can find a generic political letter dated March 12, 1947, that begins with "Dear Mrs. Homemaker"; the letter asks if she wants to be able to purchase colored margarine. At the time, the Ohio Margarine Law forbade margarine manufacturers to add any color to their product, leaving it white. The letter urged homemakers to get their state representatives to vote for Senate Bill No. 51 to repeal this prohibition. A political sign accompanying this letter urged Ohioans to vote Forrest W. Keysor into the Ohio General Assembly, as he would vote to repeal the hated margarine law. Keysor was born in 1908, and at this time, he lived in Norwalk. Aside from dabbling in politics, over his lifetime, he worked as a shipping clerk, assistant salesman and traffic manager. By the time of his death in 1983, he had retired to Clearwater, Florida.

Margarine has a long history of being demonized in the United States. The last federal restrictions on its production weren't lifted until 1950. Only Canada had stricter laws about its manufacture and sale. There, it was banned outright between 1886 and 1949. This synthetic food came from France. During that country's industrial revolution, so many rural folks moved to urban areas that the price of butter doubled between 1850 and 1870, as there was a lack of farmers to make it in sufficient quantities. Previously a French staple, butter had become so expensive that many couldn't afford it.

In 1869, Emperor Napoleon III offered a prize to anyone who could invent a cheaper alternative. Two years later, French chemist Hippolyte Mège-Mouriès won the prize after creating a new product whose chief ingredients were beef fat and skim milk. The name oleomargarine came from *oleum*, Latin for "beef," and "margarine" for the margaric acid found in milk. Although it is universally known as just margarine today, for many years, people called it oleo. These days, beef fat is no longer an ingredient.

Above: The Wickman House in Norwalk is where the *Norwalk Reflector* once had its offices and did its printing. It now serves as one half of the Firelands Historical Society and Laning-Young Research Center. *Photograph taken by the author.*

Left: A margarine repeal campaign poster, Firelands Historical Society and Laning-Young Research Center. *Photograph taken by the author.*

Margarine production began in the United States around 1875. It so threatened the dairy industry that, in 1881, Missouri banned it. New York followed suit in 1884, and the next year, seven more states, including Ohio, did the same. Margarine was treated like illegal drugs are today. Under such laws, a person could not produce, sell or possess margarine with the intent to sell. Violators could be fined up to $1,000, one year in jail or both.

In 1886, dairy interests from twenty-six states gathered in New York City to outline what would become the first federal law against this substance, the Oleomargarine Act of 1886. It slapped a $0.02-per-pound tax on domestic margarine and $0.15-per-pound tax on imported margarine. Manufacturers, wholesalers and retailers each had to pay a hefty annual license fee. Not content with this, states outlawed coloring margarine yellow. A surprising number of cases challenging this made their way to the U.S. Supreme Court.

Older relatives of the author hated margarine so much that, to this day, those who are still living refuse to eat it, despite the fact newer brands taste almost exactly like butter. Having come from poverty that was later exasperated by the Great Depression, both sets of the author's grandparents had to eat the stuff because butter was just too expensive for them to buy. And it is poverty that explains the desire to buy yellow margarine. There was shame attached to margarine's use, and, if colored yellow, visitors who saw it might take it for butter as long as they didn't taste it.

Starting in 1910, those places where a person could buy colored margarine had to charge a ten-cent tax. Legislators did this to make it about the same price as butter. The repeal of anti-coloring laws didn't come to the political forefront until after World War I. Since most of those affected were women and poor, they had little political power, the former group only gaining the vote in all states in 1920. The margarine industry did fight laws against it, but because of its beef content, margarine was associated with the meatpacking industry, whose reputation took a long time to recover after Upton Sinclair's 1906 book, *The Jungle*, laid bare its disgusting practices. (Sinclair was trying to expose the poor working conditions, but people focused on the way the meatpacking industry handled its product, not its employees.)

On April 30, 1947, the Ohio Senate voted twenty-three to eleven to repeal the law. Neither chamber of the Ohio General Assembly had ever voted on this issue before, and it faced greater opposition in the house because its members had closer ties to dairy interests. One reason for the sudden interest in margarine at this time was a spike in butter prices. In September 1947, for example, a pound of butter cost about one dollar versus thirty or thirty-five cents for margarine. One store in Detroit reported selling three times as much margarine as butter. But the Ohio House nonetheless killed the bill on the grounds that the state's dairy farmers needed protection, despite the fact that they couldn't meet the demand as it was. To that, newspaper columnist Richard T.F. Harding quipped, "No one seems to have considered prohibiting the sale of colored butter." The people of Ohio voted to repeal the state's margarine law in 1949.

II

JEFFERSON COUNTY

Fort Steuben

After the American Revolution, Congress informed the Natives that the British had ceded their land in the region called the Northwest Territory to the United States via the Treaty of Paris. And since most of the Natives living there had fought against the colonies, they had forfeited their right to their land. They were told that they would either have to remove themselves to Canada or kindly sign a treaty ceding some of the territory to the United States as reparations for their attacks on Americans during the war. They were disinclined to do either and couldn't grasp the idea of giving up their land under any circumstances. They would resist.

Congress continued with its plans. The Land Ordinance of 1785 determined that the Northwest Territory would be divided into townships that were six square miles subdivided into thirty-six one-mile-square parcels, which amounted to 640 acres. Congress, which had officially disbanded the army on June 2, 1784, replaced it with a limited force that was sent to the Ohio River frontier to maintain peace. Undermanned, underequipped and rarely paid, the force had a high rate of desertion. It wasn't until October 20, 1786, that Congress finally tripled the army's size, though even that wasn't enough, as soon, it needed to expand in order to put down Shays' Rebellion, a short-lived anti-tax uprising in western Massachusetts.

To protect surveying parties from hostile Natives, a fort was built. The task of constructing it was given to Major Jean François Hamtramck from the First American Regiment. His father had come from Luxemburg in 1749 and settled in Quebec, where he was a barber and wig maker. He married Marie Anne Bertin, who bore him their son, Jean, on August 14, 1754. When the Revolution broke out, young Jean headed south to join the American cause. It's possible that he decided to fight the British because his mother disliked them. Although his first language was French, he spoke English quite well. On November 21, 1776, Hamtramck was commissioned as a captain in the Fifth New York Regiment at the age of nineteen. After the war, he was one of the few to remain in the army.

Hamtramck arrived in the Northwest Territory in July 1786 with three companies of men tasked with removing and destroying the houses of White squatters in Mingo Bottom. On August 5, he met with the head of the U.S. surveyors, Thomas Hutchins, who asked for another company of men for protection. Obliging, throughout the rest of the summer and early fall, Hamtramck's force kept a mobile camp that followed the surveyors so they could be nearby if they were needed.

Hutchins was born sometime around 1730 in New Jersey's frontier, where he became an orphan before his sixteenth birthday. When the French and Indian War broke out in 1756, he served with Pennsylvanian troops as an ensign. After the war, he started a career as an Indian agent, during which time, he created detailed accounts of his travels, usually with complete maps. This work so impressed the British army that it gave him an officer's commission free of cost (in those days, most officers had to pay for the commission). Little is known about Hutchins's personal life, save for the fact that he remained a bachelor all his life and fathered three illegitimate children.

During the American Revolution, he remained with the British army and was promoted to the rank of captain. Wanting to become its senior engineer for the Gulf Coast, he traveled to London to meet with high-ranking officers to whom he planned to pitch his credentials. While there, letters from one of his longtime associates, Samuel Warton, were intercepted. Because Warton, who was then living in France, was a Patriot, Hutchins was accused of committing treason. He spent seven weeks in jail until he was released with no charges. It ended his army career.

Hutchins then traveled to Paris, where Benjamin Franklin oversaw his swearing an oath of loyalty to the United States. In May 1781, Congress bestowed upon Hutchins and Simeon de Witt the title of geographer of the United States, in which capacity Hutchins then headed up the surveying of the Northwest Territory. It was probably Hutchins who developed the survey's township-section-range system. In 1789, he planned to renounce his U.S. citizenship to become surveyor general for the Spanish king, but

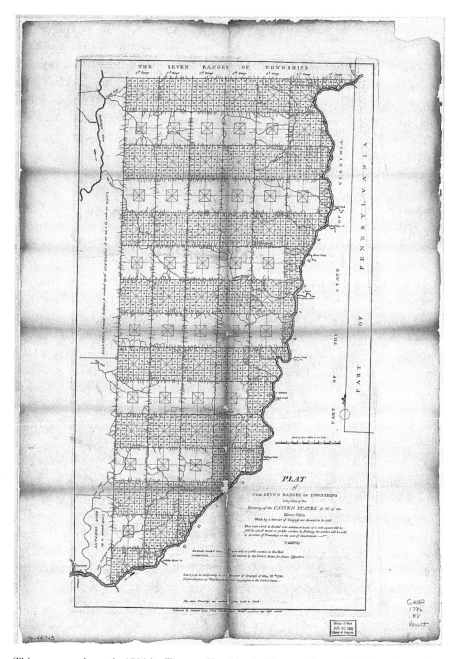

This map was drawn in 1796 by Thomas Hutchins, William Barker and Mathew Carey. It shows the first area that the surveying team covered. *Courtesy of the Library of Congress.*

he died in Pittsburgh on April 28 of that year before taking up the role. A link to the work he began was unearthed in 2012 by a road crew that was working near Brilliant on Route 7. The crew unearthed a survey stone, dated 1830, that said, "Range 2, Township 5, Section 8." It now resides on the grounds of Historic Fort Steuben, the excellent replica museum of the original structure. This is doubly appropriate, as Fort Steuben housed the nation's first federal land office.

Hamtramck still had to build a permanent fort, the site of which he had chosen. This new structure consisted of four walls and a blockhouse on each corner, these being two stories high with gun ports in the upper level. They were positioned to allow crossfire against any incoming foes. The lower part of each blockhouse served as the barracks that housed twenty-eight enlisted men crammed into a twenty-five-square-foot space. To motivate his men to build faster, Hamtramck offered six gallons of liquor to the first unit to complete its barracks. Eight days later, all of the barracks were ready. The final construction on the fort was finished on January 2, 1787. Hamtramck decided to not name the fort after himself, as suggested by his commanding officer, Colonel Josiah Harmar; instead, he named it in honor of Friedrich Wilhelm Augustus von Steuben, the Prussian officer who, during the terrible winter at Valley Forge, shaped General George Washington's men into a professional army.

With Valley Forge in mind and knowing Congress didn't always deliver promised supplies, Hamtramck hired Andrew van Swearingen as the fort's designated hunter to ensure a supply of meat a month before construction. This turned out to be a fortuitous decision, as the man who was contracted in Pittsburgh to supply food, Daniel Britt, didn't always deliver. The first beef to arrive at the fort did so under its own power on September 19, 1796.

The enlisted men were underpaid, undersupplied and under snow. In November, about two and half feet of snow had fallen around them. They were also cold. The only heat they had was a fireplace, a very inefficient way to heat a room. Most enlisted men came from America's lower classes, and the officers came from its upper classes. Many of the latter thought little of their men, and to instill discipline, they generously employed the cat-o'-nine-tails, a short whip with nine cords that could slice up a man's back in just a few strokes.

One would think that the open-minded founding fathers, whose love of personal liberty had prompted them to rebel against their king and write the Declaration of Independence, would have outlawed such a heinous instrument, but this was not the case. During the American Revolution,

Historic Fort Steuben in Steubenville is a replica of the original. *Photograph taken by the author.*

Massachusetts limited the number of lashes one man could receive to forty, as it was the maximum number allowed by Deuteronomy 25:3. The Continental Congress also adopted this limit, but Washington felt the number was too low, so he had Congress raise it to one hundred. Unsatisfied with the result—Washington didn't understand that not only is corporal punishment ineffective, it's a form of torture and abuse—in 1781, he asked Congress to raise the limit to five hundred, but Congress refused. Hamtramck also thought one hundred strokes was insufficient.

Victims of floggings needed medical attention. The fort did have a hospital, complete with a well-to-do doctor from Philadelphia who lived in a nice house across the river. But upon seeing the instruments he used for treatment, one wonders if anyone willingly sought out his help. After all, in the days before anesthesia, who would willingly subject themselves to a hot iron to cauterize the ends of blood vessels or allow someone to stick a dilator up their urethra (this often being used in cases of gonorrhea)?

Most of the officer corps under the Articles of Confederation came from Connecticut, Massachusetts, New Jersey, New York and Pennsylvania. Nearly all officers were veterans of the American Revolution and independently wealthy, allowing them to live much better lives than the enlisted men under their command. They were allotted quarters that they

Historic Fort Steuben's commissary. *Photograph taken by the author.*

shared with the surveyors. These quarters included a kitchen stocked with better food than what the enlisted soldiers had, much of it purchased with their personal funds.

As the commanding officer, Hamtramck had his own bedroom, complete with a collapsible bed surrounded by a curtain. The bed was covered with a woolen blanket produced by the Hudson Bay Company. If that didn't fend off the cold, Hamtramck's copper bed warmer likely did. He worked at a portable desk and relieved himself in a chamber pot that was emptied by his aid.

Hamtramck was ordered to abandon Fort Steuben in May 1787. By 1790, the fort had either been dismantled or burned down. Hamtramck headed to Kentucky, where he oversaw the construction of Fort Knox. He later fought alongside General Anthony Wayne at the Battle of Fallen Timbers. It was during his time with Wayne that Hamtramck was promoted to lieutenant colonel. Next, he oversaw the construction of Fort Wayne. After being promoted to the rank of a full colonel, Hamtramck stayed on as Fort Wayne's commander until his death on April 11, 1803.

12

LAKE COUNTY

Kirtland: Former Capital of the Mormons

T he town of Kirtland took its name from Turhand Kirtland, who worked for the Connecticut Land Company as a purchasing agent. In the latter part of the 1790s, he, alongside fellow agent Joshua Stow, was tasked with surveying the section of Western Reserve that became Kirtland. From this section, Stow carved out a plot for himself that, in 1812, he traded to Christopher Crary in exchange for a Massachusetts farm. Arriving that same year, Crary was considered the settlement's first permanent resident. By the time the Mormons arrived in the 1830s, the town had been firmly established.

This new religion was founded by Joseph Smith, who was born on December 23, 1805, in Sharon, Vermont. Like the majority of people in that era, his parents were farmers, though they were not very successful ones initially. At the time of Smith's birth, they had taken to renting a farm from a relative. In 1816, they moved the family to the village of Palmyra, New York, and two years later, they purchased one hundred acres for a farm in Farmington. The Church of Latter-day Saints believes that when Joseph Smith was seventeen, the angel Moroni appeared to him to point out a spot near Palmyra, where he discovered golden tablets, or plates, that carried an ancient prophecy about America and other import messages. He found the golden tablets on September 22, 1823, though they later disappeared.

It wasn't until 1827, after he married Emma Hale, that Smith began transcribing what he had read on the tablets. At first, he dictated the writings to his wife; then he dictated them to Martin Harris. His work was published as the Book of Mormon in 1830. Smith's new religion—as that is what he had created—was founded on April 6, 1830, in the Whitmer House. For the rest of his short life, Smith continued to have divine revelations, making him a prophet.

From its beginning, Smith's new religion, originally called the Church of Christ, had a missionary mandate. Smith sent four missionaries to Missouri to preach to the Natives, but local government agents put a stop to it because they feared it would break the fragile peace they had with the Natives. Upon their return,

Joseph Smith. *Courtesy of the Library of Congress.*

the missionaries stopped in Kirtland, where they converted more people than Smith himself had so far. One of the most important converts in Kirtland was Sidney Rigdon, a man born in St. Clair, Pennsylvania, on February 19, 1793.

Rigdon was, to put it bluntly, a man who was deeply uncertain when it came to his religious convictions. He had some schooling in his youth but was largely self-taught when it came to learning grammar. He loved reading and borrowed many books, his favorite being the Bible. A gifted orator, he joined the United Baptists and became a preacher in 1817. After his mother sold his family's farm in 1819, Rigdon moved to Warren, Ohio, where he became an ordained minister. In 1821, he was appointed minister for the First Baptist Church in Pittsburgh, which he ran traditionally. His meeting with Alexander Campbell changed his theological outlook. Campbell wanted to create a primitive church similar to the one from the first century CE, an idea that sent Rigdon down the path of unorthodox ideas that upset his congregation so much that he found it prudent to resign in 1824. He then turned to tanning to make a living.

Rigdon returned to religious life, moved back to Ohio and started churches in Mantua and Mentor. Although his Mentor venture was successful, his evolving theological ideas prompted him to leave it in 1830. Former members of this congregation asked him to start a new one in Kirtland. At some point, someone gave him a Book of Mormon. Inspired, Rigdon joined the Mormons, quickly becoming a counselor to the church's First Presidency.

In 1831, Rigdon headed to New York to meet Smith in person, and while he was there, he convinced Smith to relocate the church's headquarters to Kirtland, a suggestion reinforced by one of Smith's visions. Smith directed his followers to abandon their homes and move to this new place, leaving most of them impoverished, as they hadn't had the chance to sell their houses before departing. Rigdon helped shape much of the church's early theology, one of its most important tenants being to give to those who were more in need than themselves. Although many Mormons had little to relinquish, their conviction in the importance of charity prompted them to offer all they could.

Donated items, including food, were stored in the same building that housed the Whitney Red Store, which had been built by Newel K. Whitney between 1822 and 1824. It was probably the most important secular place in Kirtland's Mormon community. For a time, Smith and his wife lived here, and their original dining room table and chairs are still on display for those who wish to find a direct connection to them. It was at a meeting in this small room that Smith became so irritated with everyone smoking and chewing tobacco that he forbade his followers from using either. He also banned alcohol.

On September 5, 1822, Whitney bought land from Peter French that was located in the area known as the flats; the East Branch of the Chagrin River flowed through this area. There, Whitney built an ashery. Asheries produced potash, an alkali that was usually extracted from burning hardwood. Locals sold their wood waste here, and it was then burned down to ashes in a kiln. These ashes were placed into vats of water to extract the alkali, which was used to make a potent lye. To further refine it, the lye went into iron kettles to be evaporated or boiled down, producing the black residue known as black salts. These, in turn, were heated in large cauldrons and melted into a single mass that, after cooling, turned a grayish pink. Some potash was further refined using special ovens to produce pearlash.

Potash was used to produce a wide variety of everyday products, including soap, tanned leather, gunpowder, paper and bleached cotton textiles. Asheries were extremely profitable. Between 1800 and 1825 in New York, Vermont, and the Lowlands of the St. Lawrence Watershed, the annual average export of potash amounted to $1 million, about 2 percent of all goods exported from the United States. Production was limited mainly to the North, because the softwood trees of the South didn't work well to produce it. Along with whiskey and wheat, potash was one of the most in-demand products shipped on the Erie Canal.

Early farmers provided asheries with much-needed wood, but they soon focused on the large-scale growing of crops. Asheries went into decline in the mid-nineteenth century, when it became more profitable to transport lumber

Joseph Smith lived for a time in the upstairs area of the Whitney Store, Historic Kirtland Village. *Photograph taken by the author.*

Inside the ashery at Historic Kirtland Village. *Photograph taken by the author.*

east via canals and railroads than to burn it up. Asheries were rendered completely obsolete in 1861 with the discovery of a massive reserve of a mineral substitute in Germany.

During Kirtland's time as the Church of the Latter-Day Saints' capital, about three thousand Mormons lived there. Smith ordered the construction of a temple that would be the Mormons' most sacred site. Dedicated in 1836, its cost of $40,000 didn't help improve Smith's follower's economic woes. To help finance it, Smith and other church leaders decided to start the Kirtland Safety Society Banking Company. Despite the fact the Ohio General Assembly refused to approve its charter, in part because a non-Mormon Kirtland banker with the support of a state senator didn't want the competition, the bank opened in January 1837. It printed far more paper money than it had specie to back it. The bank then compounded this mistake by giving out a generous number of loans.

For a time, the bank did increase Mormon wealth, but it faced mounting problems. Other banks in the area refused to accept its notes and required the businesses they served to follow suit. In an effort to run the bank out of business, a fellow named Grandison Newell organized a bank run. Then came the Panic of 1837, which killed the bank altogether. Some in Smith's flock were upset with his venture into banking, and this schism ultimately led to the split in which defectors founded the Reorganized Church of Latter-day Saints, now known as the Community of Christ. It is this splinter group that owns and runs Kirtland Temple. Non-Mormons

Kirtland's Mormon Temple, one of the most sacred Latter-day Saints houses of worship, is owned and controlled by a breakaway group. *Courtesy of the Library of Congress.*

blamed Kirtland's financial problems on Smith, forcing him and most of his followers to head to Missouri. Smith, in particular, skedaddled to avoid being arrested by the local sheriff.

Rigdon and Smith arrived in the village of Far West, Missouri, in January 1838. That summer, Rigdon gave a pair of fiery sermons, enticing Mormons to resist harassment and be independent from the state. Alarmed by his words, Mormons began fighting non-Mormons. After the Mormons attacked a Missouri militia along the Crooked River, Missouri's governor Lilburn Boggs declared the Latter-day Saints a menace, ordering that they needed to be removed from the state or exterminated. Rigdon was arrested for murder, robbery, arson and treason. At his trial, Rigdon represented himself. Employing his gifted tongue, he not only got the jury to acquit, but spectators gathered a collection of one hundred dollars for him, which he used to finance his hasty departure to Illinois, where Smith and most of the congregation had relocated.

There, Rigdon's relationship with Smith began to deteriorate. On June 27, 1844, Smith was murdered at the hands of a mob in Carthage, Illinois. Rigdon's bid to make himself the church's leader was thwarted by Brigham Young, who took the position for himself. After returning to Pittsburgh, Rigdon broke with Smith altogether, deeming him "a fallen prophet." The new church he started used the Book of Mormon, but true to character, two years later, he disbanded it.

13

LORAIN COUNTY

Wellington

When Wellington was first settled, sometime between 1818 and 1820, its founders decided on its name via a contest. A history written by Mrs. W.B. Vischer that appeared as a supplement of the June 6, 1922, edition of the *Wellington Enterprise* reported that "the citizen who would cut the longest stretch of road thru the dense wilderness" would win this contest. At least that is how it was supposed to work. But when the winner chose the name "Charlemont," no one liked it and the contest resumed. The second winner, William Welling, to chose the name "Wellington," which everyone found acceptable. He claimed the name was in honor of the Duke of Wellington, recently famous for defeating Napoleon, though it's just possible Welling had in mind to name the town after himself.

The area where Wellington now stands was once claimed by Connecticut, which considered any land to the west between the forty-first and forty-second parallels its own, including parts of Pennsylvania and New York. Connecticut ultimately gave up its claim for land in those other two states but for a time kept its Ohio territory, which stretched for 120 miles west of the Pennsylvania border. Roughly the size of present-day Connecticut, it became known as the Western Reserve. A portion at its western edge was given to Connecticut citizens who lost their homes during the Revolution to British arson. This is why Huron, Erie and parts of two other counties are known as the Firelands.

On September 5, 1794, the State of Connecticut sold all its land except for the Firelands to the Connecticut Land Company for 40 cents an acre, making the final price $1.2 million. The company called its new acquisition New Connecticut, a name that clearly didn't stick. To figure out what all it possessed so it could be divvied it up in an orderly fashion, the company sent a surveying party led by Moses Cleaveland to map it out.

The Western Reserve encompassed what are now Ashtabula, Cuyahoga, Erie, Geauga, Huron, Lake, Lorain, Mahoning, Medina, Portage, Summit and Trumbull Counties. As late as the end of 1800, the thirty-two settlements here still lacked an organized government despite the fact Ohio would become a state in 1803. On July 4, 1805, the region's Native Americans signed the Treaty of Fort Industry. In exchange for giving up all claims on Western Reserve land, the U.S. government would pay them $4,000 total in three payments plus the right to hunt and fish here.

As Whites poured into Lorain County, they began cutting down its forests in the southern and western areas to make pastures for dairy farming. With little demand for milk at this time, dairy farmers focused on producing butter and Dutch cheese, better known today as cottage cheese. This type was likely chosen because it took just twenty to thirty days to be ready for shipping to market after leaving the vat in which it was made. Vats didn't come out of nowhere, so local suppliers appeared in the area, such as Wellington's Sage's Patent Cheese Vat and Heater.

Wellington resident Doctor D.J. Johns convinced the Cleveland, Columbus, Cincinnati & St. Louis Railroad to run its tracks through the village and make it a stop. It opened in 1850 and in that year Rollin Horr became the first person to use it to ship cheese from Wellington, this having

A closeup of a map drawn in 1812 by John Melish and John Vallance that shows the Western Reserve. *Courtesy of the Library of Congress.*

come from the factory he and his brothers had built in nearby Huntington. Soon Wellington became the largest shipping point for cheese and butter in the world. Horr's brother-in-law, B.J. Carpenter, constructed the village's first cheese warehouse. By 1876 forty cheese factories operated in the area, most of it being shipped out of Wellington.

Wellington's railroad station agent reported that the total pounds in cheese shipped in 1859 was 1,084,500 and 378,854 for butter. By the turn of the twentieth century, the demand for milk in Lorain County rose to the point where it made economic sense for dairy farmers to sell this in growing cities such as Lorain, Cleveland, Akron and Elyria rather than putting all that extra effort it took to make it into cheese. Decline of its production ended Wellington's dominance as major cheese shipping center.

Wellington is home of the Spirit of '76 Museum in which one will find a display case a containing a buckskin outfit that belonged to John Alexander Justice, a man whose picture ought to be beside "eccentric" in the dictionary. Born in Lorain County's Brighton Township in 1838, he lived at the corner of Gore Orphanage Road and Route 18, about two miles outside Wellington. Twenty-three when the Civil War broke out, he never participated in that conflict.

To the community in which he lived he was known as a recluse and hoarder. He owned fifty acres of land on which he did much hunting and trapping. At the back of his cabin he had a blacksmith's shop. He collected many artifacts, especially Native American ones. He once walked all the way down to the Florida Keys, then made his way to Cuba by boat, collecting all sorts of interesting items such as guns, Indian artifacts, and antiques along the way. In all he made seven trips to Florida and the South, but these stopped when property owners began frowning on him camping and hunting on their land.

Those Justice knew well called him Alex. His parents were well educated, and he learned to write from his mother. He was of Spanish, Irish, English, and Native American descent, this last probably explaining his lifelong fascination with relics from that part of his heritage. He farmed part of his land and probably generated most of his income as a blacksmith and from the sale of furs. As a blacksmith he repaired items and made axes. His skills were varied. He was an accomplished taxidermist, crafted silver rings by melting silver coins, and built himself an octagon-shaped banjo. A generous man, he often gave his handicrafts away. For clothes he usually wore buckskin and moccasins. In the summers he lived outdoors in a camp by a wood where he cooked food in pots over an open fire. He kept a coffin in

Wellington's The Spirit of '76 Museum is in one of the town's former cheese warehouses. *Photograph taken by the author.*

his bedroom and one time showed a visitor that he fit in it. Daniel Boone was also said to have kept a coffin under his bed, lying in it every so often to make sure he still could so.

With old age came a deterioration of Justice's eyesight. One day two men came by and told him they were eye specialists who could restore it. As they examined his eyes into which they put drops, they drugged him. When he awoke, most of his antiques, artifacts and money was gone. The thieves were never caught. When he died in 1926 at the age of eighty-eight, part of his vast collection of Native American artifacts went to the Laning-Young Research Center, which is run by the Firelands Historical Society. He is buried in Brighton Cemetery.

14

MAHONING COUNTY

The Rise and Fall of the Steel Industry

Mahoning Valley became a major iron-producing region after the discovery of iron ore at Mineral Ridge and block coal at Brier Hill. By the time the local supply of both ran out, the iron and steel industries had become so well-established that they imported what they needed to continue operations. In the earliest days of the area's iron production, charcoal was the fuel of choice. When a process to mass produce steel was discovered, coke (coal with its impurities burned out) replaced charcoal because it burns hotter and makes far less smoke. As demand for steel increased and the need for iron decreased, Mahoning Valley mills adapted. When, for example, the Youngstown Iron Sheet and Tube Company in East Youngstown switched to making steel, it removed "Iron" from its name.

Mahoning Valley's industrial might attracted immigrants who were fresh off the boat. Many of them moved to Youngstown (not be confused with the aforementioned East Youngstown, which, from here on out, will be called by its modern name of Campbell), causing its population to grow by fifteen thousand between 1900 and 1912. An influx of Black emigrants fleeing the Jim Crow South significantly changed Youngstown's demographics. In 1900, they made up mere 2 percent of the population, and most of them didn't work in the city's industries, but between 1910 and 1920, their population increased by a staggering 244 percent.

In the first few decades of the twentieth century, demand for housing in Youngstown far outstripped supply. This was made worse by a lack of mass transit, forcing workers to live within walking distance of their place of employment. Much of Youngstown's considerable immigrant population wasn't even allowed to rent because the owners of these properties preferred wealthier tenants. The housing that was available to immigrants was mainly concentrated in the business district. There, the rent was still too high to pay, causing several families to cram themselves into single-family residences. It was not unusual for those in this situation to sleep in shifts. By 1912, about fifteen thousand were working in the city's mills, furnaces and shops. Many residences lacked running water, and people took in lodgers to supplement their incomes. Another barrier to buying a home was a lack of a mortgage system, meaning even better-paid workers couldn't hope to save enough to buy a house outright.

When housing was studied by the Charity Organization Society, it found conditions unsanitary. So, in 1909, it set up the Modern Homes Company to build and sell affordable homes. It bought about seven acres in Youngstown, where it constructed houses surrounding a park. Using cinder blocks, the company's structures went up quickly. The houses had bathrooms, running water, light fixtures and heating via natural gas. In 1911, Modern Homes began building better-quality homes that it sold using a mortgage system.

The lack of sufficient housing persisted well the 1930s. To help alleviate the problem, Youngstown constructed houses in what it called Westlake Terrace. This community was opened in August 1939. During the Great Depression, the U.S. government started promoting home ownership, first with a VA program and then with the introduction of the Federal Housing Administration that backed private loans to make banks more willing to give them out.

Between 1915 and 1930, between 1.5 and 2 million Black emigrants left the Jim Crow South to go to the urban North, which didn't go over well with the White residents who were living in the latter. They were just as racist as their southern brethren and resented having to compete with Black residents for housing. Northern U.S. cities created segregated neighborhoods using legal tools, such as zoning and deed restrictions. The White people who controlled housing and real estate believed that integration would devalue their properties, and they held the racist belief that non-White people didn't add value their neighborhoods. As a result, bankers refused to give Black residents loans, and real estate boards forbade their agents from renting or selling to Black residents in White areas.

A lack of housing was just one of the many grievances that workers in Mahoning Valley, particularly the immigrants and Black residents, had.

Low-skill workers suffered from insufficient wages and oppressive company-run private police forces. On December 27, 1915, workers at Republic Steel went on strike for higher wages. Those at Youngstown Sheet and Tube followed. The latter company brought in strike breakers, and just after 6:00 p.m. on January 7, 1916, about two thousand strikers jeered these scabs as they left for the day. The head of Youngstown Sheet and Tube's private police force, J.M. Woltz, ordered his men to attack the strikers.

In response, the workers, many of them Austrians, rioted. Arming themselves with revolvers and dirks, the workers set fire to one of the company's office buildings and then moved into Campbell's business district. There, they looted and burned all the saloons except one, which they entered, demanding the barkeep serve them drinks. When the barkeep refused, the workers threw him out the window and helped themselves.

An article from the January 8 edition of the newspaper *Daybook* reported this scene of anarchy:

> *Police and sheriffs' deputies endeavored to quell the riot the strike guards had brought about, but they were unable to cope with the situation. Electric light wires were cut, and a hose was slashed when firemen tried to put out the flames. Barrels of whisky were rolled into the street, and men drank, forming cups with their hands. Five hundred pounds of dynamite were taken from a freight car by the men and improvised into bombs, which were hurled into buildings. The postoffice [sic] building was burned after one man was seen ransacking the place. None of the contents were saved. The International bank [sic] was burned. Twenty foreign [immigrant] families were made homeless by the spread of flames, which were carried from roof to roof by high wind. When flames communicated with Schoenfeld jewelry store [sic], a crowd broke in into it and stole $5,000 worth of jewelry. Diamonds glittered on grimy hands. Jewels worth hundreds of dollars were carried or carelessly pinned on coats.*

The fires spread for blocks, and they, along with the vandalism did an estimated $800,000 worth of damage. The number of deaths was between one and three. One man was shot and killed while looting a store. Nineteen people, including a woman, were injured, and at least fifteen buildings were burned. State troopers were called in to restore order.

An agreement between the strikers and Youngstown Sheet and Tube was reached on January 12, 1916. Workers asked for a raise from nineteen

The Ohio militia patrols Campbell in the aftermath of the riots. *Courtesy of the Library of Congress.*

and a half cents to twenty-five cents an hour, and they got twenty-two cents, about a 10 percent increase for semiskilled and skilled workers. The company began the construction of 281 row houses that immigrants and Black workers could rent for as little as fifteen dollars a month. Their roofs were made from clay tiles, and their walls were made of concrete; this made them both fire resistant and durable.

Authorities didn't let the riot go unpunished. United States district attorney Ed. S. Wertz issued arrest warrants for three of the riot's alleged ringleaders. Post Office Inspector George Pate investigated the attack on postal property and had suspects for whom he wanted arrest warrants issued. Those who were apprehended would be charged with the looting and the destruction of Campbell's post office.

The Committee on Industrial Relations issued a report that laid blame for the initial strike on wages that were so low, one couldn't live on them. About 70 percent of the workers were recent immigrants who earned less than $500 a year. During lean times, Youngstown Steel and Tube would go down to three-day weeks, depressing earnings even further; yet, the company still paid its shareholders dividends. During such times, the company gave men with families baskets of food and then deducted the cost from their next paycheck.

The Ohio Federation of Labor (OFL) determined that Youngstown Sheet and Tube brought the strike and riot on itself. Workers were forced to work twelve-hour days seven days a week. The company did not offer its largely immigrant workforce any kind of education, and only a few of the workers' children went to school. The OFL also blamed steamship companies for luring these workers to America under false pretenses so that they could be exploited. This was an ongoing problem in the early twentieth century.

In an attempt to ease tensions and prevent powerful outside organized labor groups from making inroads, many of the Mahoning Valley's companies started offering generous benefits. These included, according to an informational sign at the Youngstown Historical Center of Industry and Labor, "employee stock-purchasing plans, compensation for accident victims, company-subsidized housing, retirement pensions, safety programs, sanitary washrooms, the adoption of the eight-hour day and company unions," though these unions weren't independent. When the Great Depression came, nearly all of these benefits disappeared until the Steel Workers Organizing Committee was founded on June 17, 1936, in Pittsburgh. Its first contract granted a five-dollar-a-day minimum salary, plus things we take for granted today, including the forty-hour week, overtime paid as time-and-a-half, seniority and the introduction of a system in which one could issue a grievance.

When the United States entered World War II after the bombing of Pearl Harbor, Mahoning Valley and its steel mills became especially critical to the war effort. They were so important that Hollywood star Marlene Dietrich arrived in Youngstown on Monday, June 22, 1942, to hawk war bonds. Born in Schöneberg, Germany, on December 27, 1901, Marie Magdalene Dietrich was the daughter of an imperial police officer. In April 1930, at the age of twenty-nine, three years before Hitler became Germany's dictator, Dietrich departed for Hollywood. By the time World War II war broke out, Dietrich was a U.S. citizen. When her attempts to reach the people she knew in Germany failed, she began listening to the radio to get as much European news as she could. America's desire to stay out of the war upset her.

After the United States entered the war, she enthusiastically put her energy toward selling war bonds, going so far as to sell kisses and visit nightclubs, activities President Franklin D. Roosevelt disapproved of. Though she hated Hitler, she feared that her efforts were paying for bombs that might kill her loved ones in Germany. The flood of refugees fleeing the war horrified her. As they arrived in America, she gave them food, money and jobs if possible.

When Dietrich came to Youngstown, she brought with her a motorcade that was greeted by Mayor William B. Spagnola. At Central Square, she

Alfred T. Palmer, *Steel Production*, Office of War Information. *Courtesy of the Library of Congress.*

was greeted by ten thousand people and serenaded by the Navy Club Boy's Band. She lunched at Youngstown Club and then toured several factories, including Youngstown Sheet and Tube. She stressed that the workers' contribution to the war effort was far more important than hers.

After the war, America's steel production accounted for 63.7 percent of the world's supply of steel. In the fall of 1959, a massive strike over work rules began and lasted for 116 days. Nearly half a million workers participated, making it the largest work stoppage in American history. Some consider it the opening foreign steel makers needed to get into the U.S. market, but the truth was that foreign steel had already gotten in. Japanese steel imports, for example, went from 31,466 tons in 1957 to a 4.5 million tons just ten years later. Japanese steel was just as good if not better than American steel and cost about 15 percent less. So, how did Republic, Bethlehem and U.S. Steel respond? They raised their prices to keep profits high.

The decline of the American steel industry can be laid squarely at the feet of those who ran these companies. In 1959, R. Conrad Cooper of U.S. Steel came up with a plan in eight points that would break the unions,

Photographer Alfred T. Palmer took this somewhat impressionist photograph for the Office of War Information in 1941 at Republic Steel in Youngstown. *Courtesy of the Library of Congress.*

the idea being that the resulting wage cuts and benefits would increase profits. This is what motivated the leaders of the U.S. steel industry to stop upgrading the equipment in their mills, as they figured they would get all they could out of their mills and then shut them down when they were too obsolete to be profitable.

After steel companies raised prices seven years in a row, makers of tin cans started looking for an alternative and found it in aluminum. Bethlehem and U.S. Steel did reduce the price of their tin, but when aluminum makers Reynolds Metals Company and Alcoa lowered their prices, the two steel companies decided to shut down their production of tin for cans altogether, despite the fact it brought in $2 billion a year. Car manufacturers began replacing steel parts in cars, such as dome lights, instrument panels and grills with plastic.

The big steel makers met this challenge by doing pretty much nothing. Their research and development were weak and uninterested in great leaps forward. Bethlehem Steel didn't even bother to invest in the basic oxygen furnace that reduced the time it took to make steel. The company had been put off by technical issues that were soon overcome by the Japanese and West Germans. This wasn't the only new piece of technology the company refused to adopt.

All of these factors caused the amount of American-made steel in the world market to drop to a mere 11.1 percent in 1985. The devastation of the Mahoning Valley began on September 1, 1977, with the closure of Youngstown Sheet and Tube Mill, which its owner, the LTV Corporation, decided wasn't worth modernizing. Known as "Black Monday," about five thousand lost their jobs in the weeks after the announcement. Over the next eight years, four more mills were shuttered. In the 1950s, ten steel mills had operated in the Mahoning Valley.

Local politicians did nothing. It was Bishop James W. Malone who organized a movement to deal with the crisis. An alliance of out-of-work laborers, political radicals and religious leaders formed the Ecumenical Coalition of the Mahoning Valley. It publicized the region's plight and made an attempt to reopen the Campbell Works that were owned and operated by the community. It even convinced the Department of Housing and Urban Development to look into it, but nothing came of the effort when President Jimmy Carter's administration declined to offer an important loan guarantee. Today, just a few steel producers operate in Mahoning Valley.

15

MEDINA COUNTY

Lake Shore Electric Railway Company

T here was a time when Northeast Ohio was crisscrossed with electric-powered trolley systems that could take a person just about anywhere they needed to go. Most of those systems have disappeared off the face of the earth without a trace, but some of the streetcars from them have found a new home in Medina County's Northern Ohio Railway Museum. Of these streetcars, quite a few belonged to the once-mighty interurban Lake Shore Electric Railway Company (LSE).

Systems that connected towns and cities became known as interurbans, a term coined in 1892 by Congressman Charles L. Henry from Indiana. The first electric interurban trolley began operating in 1892, connecting North Anderson and South Anderson in Indiana. But because the line only spanned two miles, most historians consider Oregon East Side Railway's fifteen-mile connection between Portland and Oregon City to be the first true interurban. East Side was founded by brothers James and George Steel in 1892. The company's first car, *Helen*, departed for its maiden trip on February 16, 1893. Its electric power was generated by water. Though it became the template for other successful lines, it didn't do very well itself. Before its first year of operation ended, it went into receivership, and by 1898, its track was in bad shape.

In the late nineteenth and early twentieth centuries, electric interurbans were the cheapest, best way to travel in and between towns and cities. The LSE system didn't start from scratch; rather, it was a consolidation of four existing systems that were bought by the Everett-Moore Syndicate. Capitalized at $4

Lake Shore Electric Railway car, Northern Ohio Railway Museum. *Photograph taken by the author.*

million, with its main office in Cleveland, the deal to purchase the last of the companies was closed on March 1, 1901. The combined system had about 130 miles of track. Integrating four formally independent systems was not easy. It took several years and quite a bit of investment to make it happen.

Once fully operational, its main line ran from Cleveland to Toledo, primarily along Lake Erie's shore, though it veered farther south to include smaller communities, such as Norwalk, Monroeville, Bellevue and Clyde. It connected to other trolley systems that took passengers as far west as Fort Wayne, Indiana; south to Lima, Ohio, and north to Detroit, Michigan. Despite the cost of the merger, by 1906, LSE had turned a profit, reporting that it sold 4,761,000 fares, took in $860,000 in gross profits and finished off with a $136,514 profit for that year. By World War I, LSE was operating 180 miles of its own track, just a sliver of Ohio's 2,800 miles of interconnected tracks.

In the late nineteenth century, electrification was spotty across America and was not always reliable. Cleveland was an early adopter of electrification for its streetlights, hotels and trolleys, but growing cities like it had little trouble finding the financing and users to make it profitable. Small towns in rural areas had to either generate power themselves or get it from a larger city, both options usually being cost prohibitive. Fortunately, the electric grid came to them due to the LSE's need for electricity between Toledo and Cleveland.

The author's grandmother, born in 1912 on a farm outside of Norwalk, used this system. When compared to traveling by car today, it was by no means a speedy way to travel, especially since it had frequent stops at stations along its routes. It took, for example, about an hour and fifty minutes to travel from Norwalk to Sandusky, a total of eighteen miles. LSE wasn't the only available mass transit system. The Norwalk & Mansfield Railway took passengers from Norwalk, to Sandusky, North Fairfield, Steuben and Mansfield. A spur connected the line to Chicago Junction, which is now Willard.

As a child, the author was always told to never stick his hands or head out of the window of a moving vehicle, or he might lose them. While the odds of this happening are pretty low, they aren't negligible. In September 1907, twenty-year-old Otis Ottney, a carpenter from Gibsonburg, learned this the hard way. One Sunday, he, along with his seventeen-year-old brother, Garth, and two friends, decided to spend the day in Toledo. At around 11:00

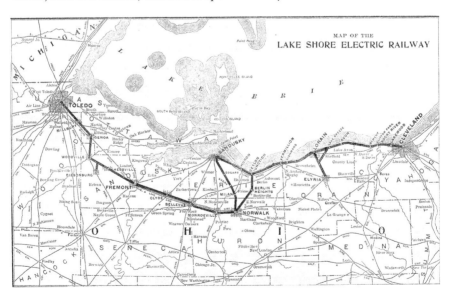

This Lake Shore Electric Railway map is from 1906 edition of the *Commercial and Financial Chronicle. Courtesy of the Internet Archive.*

p.m., Ottney stuck his head out the window of LSE Coach 61 to speak to a passenger on the other side of the car's internal partition that divided its smoking and nonsmoking sections. Unnoticed by him was the Maumee Valley Car No. 726 that was coming from the other direction.

As the cars passed one another, he was pulled out of his car and squeezed into the four inches between them. The newspaper article from the September 20 edition of the *Perrysburg Journal* spared no details: "Passengers of both cars were startled by a sharp scream, followed by the crunching of bones, and they were horrified to see the body of Ottney disappearing through the window. So horrible was the sight of spurting blood and the grinding of bones as Ottney's body was being crushed and drawn between the cars that several women fainted." Ottney was stretched across ten feet of track, and it took a good number of men to pull his remains back into the car through another window.

In May 1910, Jim Cullium, an employee of the Nickel Plate Railroad from Bellevue, used the LSE to take off with fifteen-year-old Leah Presti. She was the sister-in-law of Culium's friend, Blaggio Cressi, and Culium ran off with her because he'd fallen in love. He had offered her $500 to walk with him, and during the stroll, he proposed marriage. To this, she consented, and the two, along with her brother Jimmie, boarded an LSE train headed to Cleveland. When he was arrested in Cleveland on the charge of kidnapping—as that is what it amounted to—Cullium was also fined $100 for carrying a concealed revolver.

LSE profits peaked in 1920. In 1923, the Cleveland-Lorain Highway Coach Company began operating a rival bus route that, by 1927, had seriously cut into the LSE's ridership. Improved highways and low-cost automobiles also reduced the number of people who needed to use the system. On March 23, 1927, the company announced a reorganization. Cities Service Company bought control of the LSE by investing $800,000 into it, but by the end of the year, its Norwalk-Milan-Sandusky route had lost so much revenue that its trolleys were replaced with buses. The line's tracks began falling into disrepair along with other parts of the infrastructure, and by 1938, they were shut down completely.

LSE wasn't the only streetcar line to fail around this time. Many books and articles have covered the conspiracy of General Motors, Standard Oil of California and Firestone to buy and rip up streetcar lines across America in an effort to force people to buy cars and cities to buy buses. This conspiracy is often referred to as the General Motors Trolley Conspiracy. This was just a small part of the issue, and the real culprit for the streetcar system's decline was President Franklin D. Roosevelt. In 1935, he signed the Public Utility Company Holding Act (PUCHA), also known as the Wheeler-Rayburn Act, that forced power companies to divest of their other ventures. PUCHA was a reaction to the collapse of Samuel Insull's massive utility holding company. Because most electric streetcar companies were owned by power companies that could subsidize them if they became unprofitable, after the power companies divested of their streetcar systems, many of these mass transit organizations went out of business in a short time.

In 1920, garage owner E. Roy Fitzgerald, who had a seventh-grade education, started a small bus company in Eveleth, Minnesota, called Range Rapid Transit. He, along with his brothers, grew the business, and in 1936, it morphed into the powerful National City Lines (NCL). Obtaining credit and money from GM and its silent partners, Standard Oil, Mack Truck and Firestone, NCL bought up all sorts of then-orphaned streetcar lines, and in many cases, it ripped up the tracks and replaced them with buses, though, in Philadelphia and Los Angeles, it continued to operate the existing streetcars.

NCL purchased sixty-two streetcar companies in the 1930s and 1940s, but this wasn't necessarily a burden on those who used those streetcars. By this time, many Americans preferred cars as their primary means of transportation because they freed them from the restriction of route schedules. Those who still used mass transit often preferred buses because they were more comfortable than streetcars. This isn't to say the conspiracy didn't exist. NCL, GM and seven other companies were fined $5,000 each for creating a monopoly to sell fuel, tires and buses, and seven executives were fined a whopping $1 each for their part in it.

16

PORTAGE COUNTY

Kent

In 1780, several years before the founding of what would one day become the city of Kent, an interesting incident occurred in this location. General Daniel Brodhead, then in charge of Fort Pitt, sent Captain Samuel Brady to Ohio's Lower Sandusky (now Fremont) region to spy on the Native and British forces assembling there. Brady's upbringing made him perfect for this assignment. Born in May 1756 and raised in Pennsylvania's Susquehanna Valley, he grew up side by side with Natives, and from them, he learned much about their ways, including how to imitate wolf howls and turkey clucks. During the American Revolution, Brady's regiment, the Eighth Pennsylvania, was sent to Fort Pitt, where it guarded against possible incursions from the Iroquois, a British ally. There, Brady, then a lieutenant, commanded scouts who dressed themselves as Natives.

On August 7, 1778, a party of Seneca and Munsee killed Brady's brother close to where Loyalsock Creek emptied into the Susquehanna River. Brady's father was killed by Natives in an ambush. Brady had no problem setting up ambushes of his own to exact revenge. When he heard that Natives had attacked a family and taken their ten-year-old girl and twelve-year-old boy, he was determined to rescue them. With the aid of a Native guide, he and twenty men tracked down the perpetrators and launched a surprise attack on them in the morning, killing all seven. The boy asked to see Brady's tomahawk and used it to lop the head off of one of his captors. The children were brought to Pittsburgh, where they were reunited with their father, who had been away when the raiding party struck.

For his venture to scout the Lower Sandusky area, Brady brought with him four rangers and Chickasaw guides. Things didn't go well. All, save for Brady, were captured. He made a southeastward run for it with a party of Natives in pursuit. Upon reaching the Cuyahoga River at the spot where Kent now stands, it appeared the he had nowhere else to run. Undaunted, he leaped to the far bank, which was lower by three feet on the other side. He landed about five feet beneath its crest, then scrambled up to its top. The stunned Natives started shooting at him, one of their rifle shots hitting him in the right thigh. He made his way to a nearby lake that has since taken his name, and there, he hid underwater while breathing through a reed until the next night. One presumes that he didn't stay underwater the whole time, only when necessary. After his pursuers departed, he walked back to Pittsburgh.

A look at the place where he made his famous leap would lead the average person to dismiss it as impossible, but what you see today is much different from when Brady encountered. The river was widened in 1840, when the Pennsylvania and Ohio Canal's engineers dammed it to create slack water. They also modified one of the banks to build a towpath. In Brady's day, it was twenty-two feet across, not an impossible distance, especially for a man fleeing for his life. At the time of this writing, the longest recorded jump by human being is twenty-nine feet and two and a half inches, made by Bob Beamon during the 1968 Summer Olympics.

Brady continued to have an exciting life, doing things such as scouting along the Redbank Creek, rescuing the Gray family, spying on Natives and nearly being burned at the stake. All of this must have taken a serious toll on him. He died at the age of thirty-nine on December 25, 1795, of pleurisy, a painful disease in which the lungs fill up with fluid.

In 1798, Aaron Olmstead purchased the land that would one day become Kent, though he named it Franklin after his son. The first settler to buy land from him and settle there was Jacob Haymaker in 1805. A carpenter and millwright by trade, Haymaker had come from Pennsylvania. When his sons Frederick and George arrived the next year, the three constructed a dam on the Cuyahoga River and built a gristmill. They called their fledging settlement Riedsburg, but it became known as Franklin Mills.

The Haymakers sold their mill in 1811 but didn't abandon the place they had established. Frederick partnered with Joshua Woodward, who came to town in 1818, and, with him, set up a small wool and die factory, built houses and established Woodward's Tavern. Although their partnership dissolved in 1826, Woodward continued to develop the community with investments in

Frank T. Merrill illustration of Samuel Kenton hiding in the water that appeared in Albert F. Blaisdell and Francis K. Ball's *Pioneers of America*. *Digitized by Google Books.*

its mills. He also made his personal residence a stop on the Underground Railroad, one of the several in town.

In the late 1820s or early 1830s, a Ravenna businessman named Zenas Kent arrived in town. The father of thirteen children, some of whom would shape his new home's history, Kent controlled much of the water rights on the Cuyahoga River's shore, owned a good deal of property and founded several businesses, such as Kent National Bank. In 1835, he decided to start a tannery, and to that end, he invited a fellow named John Brown (of Harpers Ferry fame) to become his partner in the venture.

Deeming Brown too erratic to run the new venture, Zenas put his son Marvin in charge. It failed to make a much money, so Marvin converted it into a warehouse in 1844. The

This daguerreotype of John Brown, taken around 1850, was later photographed by Levin C. Handy. *Courtesy of the Library of Congress.*

property remained in the Kent family until 1923. In the 1950s and 1960s, it became part of a salvage yard. Although it was put in the National Registry of Historic Places in 1973, the city of Kent condemned it. A legal battle over its fate ensued in which the city prevailed. It was finally torn down in 1976. The land on which it once stood is now the John Brown Tannery Park.

Marvin was as enterprising as his father and started several factories and mills that made items such as woolens, flour and glass. While constructing yet another factory for cotton production, Marvin decided that a railroad going through town was an excellent way to transport his products. Seeing a need to connect the New York & Erie Railroad with the Ohio & Mississippi Railroad, he asked the Ohio General Assembly to give him a charter, which it did on March 10, 1851. The title that was given to him for the new road was the Coal Hill Railroad, named as such to keep lobbyists from discerning its true purpose and interfering. When its charter was issued, it took the name Franklin & Warren Railroad Company, but once construction got underway in July 1853, it changed its name to Atlantic & Great Western Railroad (A&GW). Marvin became its first president.

The year before, on October 8, representatives from several railroads, including the A&GW and the New York & Erie, met at the American Hotel in Cleveland to discuss connecting the cities of Philadelphia and Erie to

the existing roads by building a new line in Pennsylvania. Financed by the partnered roads, it would create a north–south route between Meadville to Erie. The Panic of 1857 derailed the financing, so money had to be found overseas, one source being a Spanish nobleman who bought $1 million in bonds. Money ran out again, so company representatives once again went overseas for funding.

Although the extension road finally got built, it caused the A&GW to go bankrupt in 1867. After reorganizing and consolidating, the former head of the Union army during the Civil War, George B. McClellan, became a major owner and the company's president. He was no more successful at this than he'd been at leading the North to victory, and on December 10, 1874, the road went into receivership again. Finally, in 1896, the Erie Railroad (it had dropped "New York" from its name in 1861) bought the A&GW outright.

Franklin Mills changed its name to Kent on May 6, 1867, when the Ohio General Assembly approved its incorporation as a village. The town wanted to thank Marvin for bringing the railroad. The town's post office had been calling it Kent since 1864. In 1867, the A&GW established a boxcar construction yard in town that gave two hundred people good jobs. By the turn of the twentieth century, it had been shuttered, and most of the town's railroad jobs were gone. The town needed to find another source for well-paying jobs. It decided to pay its primary and secondary teachers a generous wage in an effort to attract the best, giving its school system an excellent reputation that, in turn, attracted many industries and businesses to Kent because they knew they would find a well-educated workforce.

Kent State Normal School, 1914 summer term class photograph. *Courtesy of the Library of Congress.*

Education of a different sort ensured the town's future prosperity. On May 10, 1910, the Ohio General Assembly passed a bill that established two normal schools—the name then used for institutions of higher learning that were dedicated to producing schoolteachers—one in the northwest and one in the northeast. A commission chose Kent as the location for the northeastern school, thanks to the generous donation of fifty acres of land by one of Zenas's grandsons, William S. Kent. The school was named Kent State Normal School. The first two buildings that were erected were Merrill Hall for classes and Lowry Hall for dormitories. Over the years, the school's curriculum expanded beyond teaching, so it changed its name to Kent State University to reflect this.

A terrible event occurred at the school on May 4, 1970, when the U.S. National Guard opened fired on a crowd of students who were protesting the Vietnam War. Four students died, and nine were injured. The shooting occurred at 12:20 p.m., when tired and scared national guardsmen reacted to being harassed by a small contingent of militant students. Twenty-eight guardsmen unleashed a hail of bullets; the shooting lasted for thirteen seconds as their officers frantically tried to stop them. Sandy Scheuer, William Schroeder, Allison Krause and Jeffrey Miller were all killed. Of those students, only Miller had harassed the guardsmen. Dean Kahler was struck in the back, paralyzing him for life. This incident helped firmly turn the country against the war. It so horrified Neil Young that he penned the Crosby, Stills, Nash & Young song "Ohio" in protest.

17

RICHLAND COUNTY

Mansfield

W hen Prohibition began in 1919, the man tasked with enforcing it, John F. Kramer, temporarily set up his headquarters in Mansfield after President Wilson appointed him as the federal Prohibition commissioner on November 12, 1919. A lawyer and former Ohio state legislator known as "Honest John" Kramer spent his first ten days as commissioner on the second floor over the Walk-Over Shoe Store on Main Street before moving to Washington, D.C. He oversaw the nation's Prohibition efforts, though it was generally left up to the states to enforce Prohibition. He served as commissioner for about a year and a half until the next president, Republican Warren G. Harding, replaced him with his own man. During his tenure, Kramer created some of the loopholes that allowed people to acquire alcohol legally, such as it being considered medicine when prescribed by a doctor.

Mansfield, like the rest of America, was divided over support for Prohibition, though temperance had a long history in the city. The first temperance movement there was started around 1828. But since the town at this time had a large population of Germans, for whom beer was part of their culture, the city became known for this beverage. When anti-alcohol crusader Carry Nation came to town in 1902, there were at least fifty-one saloons in operation. A number of Mansfield brewers, including Frank & Son Brewery and the Renner & Weber Brewing Company, kept them supplied. Mansfield's first brewer, John Wiler, began making beer for his hotel in 1821. This was probably ale, which was not all that popular in America at this time, nor did it have a long shelf life.

It was the influx of German immigrants into America that introduced lager, the lighter, foaming beer Americans prefer today. Unlike ale, which could be produced quickly, lager needed to age, sometimes as long as three months, and it required near-freezing temperatures, which explains why early breweries stored it underground. Once out of cold storage, it didn't last long, so brewers only delivered what was needed, limiting the range in which it could be sold.

John F. Kramer was the United States' first federal Prohibition commissioner. He briefly set up his headquarters over a shoe store in Mansfield. *Courtesy of the Library of Congress.*

Artificial refrigeration using ice began in earnest after the Civil War, but getting beer to faraway markets still wasn't possible until the introduction of the refrigerated car and the massive postwar boom in railroads. Track mileage increased from 53,000 to 164,000 miles between 1865 and 1895. Since large numbers of Germans had settled in the Midwest, it stood to reason that these brewers were the ones to expand nationally. Anheuser-Busch out of St. Louis, Missouri, for example, jumped from producing 44,961 gallons in 1871 to 1 million in 1901, making it one of the largest brewers in the United States.

The Mansfield Memorial Museum had an exhibit about the city's numerous now-defunct breweries and the effect of Prohibition on the city when the author visited in 2019. This is the oldest museum in Richland County. It's housed in the Soldiers and Sailors Memorial Building, which was constructed in 1888. During the late nineteenth and early twentieth centuries, Ohio built thirteen memorial buildings in honor of its soldiers and sailors. The first constructed was this one, and it's also the last standing that is still being used for its original purpose. Ohio stopped building memorial buildings after World War I, when the VFW and American Legion began erecting halls in which veterans could meet.

It was there, on the second floor, that the Civil War veterans' association called the Grand Army of the Republic met. The Memorial Library Association (now the Mansfield/Richland County Library) installed itself in the first floor, where it stayed until 1908. On the third floor was the Mansfield Memorial Museum, which was founded by Edward Wilkinson, who served as its first full-time curator until July 18, 1905. During his

This exhibit in the Mansfield Memorial Museum shows a number of artifacts from the city's heyday of beer production. *Photograph taken by the author.*

tenure, he labeled much of the collection and built the glass cabinets in which many artifacts are still displayed. Under his curatorship, it became one of the best museums in the Midwest.

Though forgotten today, Wilkinson was well known in the nineteenth century scientific community for his collection of amphibians and reptiles that he'd gathered from the Mexican state of Chihuahua. Born in Mansfield in 1846, his first career was that of sheet metal worker, but he took a break to fight in the Civil War. In 1873, his brother invited him to work in Chihuahua at the mine he ran. During his two years there, Wilkinson collected many specimens, returning in 1885 to find more.

He, along with several others, including Dr. J.R. Craig, combined their personal collections to create the Mansfield Memorial Museum, which opened its doors on October 12, 1891. Founding a museum using one's own personal collection was not unusual in the eighteenth and nineteenth centuries. One example of this is the Egyptian Hall in London. Located on the southern side of Piccadilly Circus, it was built in 1812, and, as its name suggests, it looked like an Egyptian tomb, complete with hieroglyphics that no one could read at

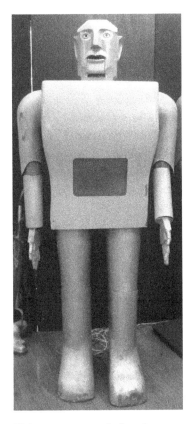

Elektro was a marvel of analog engineering in its day, Mansfield Memorial Museum. *Photograph taken by the author.*

the time. G.F. Robinson built this edifice for a staggering £16,000, a sound investment, as it turned out.

Since Egyptian Hall was built as a natural history museum, some of its first items on display included a lion, giraffe, elephant and birds, all stuffed. It also had art, fossils and weapons. Its core collection came from the items William Bullock had amassed over thirty years of travel in Central America. Beyond his contribution, the museum also drew on the collections of Sir Aston Lever and the Litchfield Museum. The museum's popularity peaked in 1816, when it put Napoleon's carriage on display. This attracted ten thousand people daily. In 1819, its collection was auctioned off. After that, the building was used primarily as a theater and exhibition hall until its demolition in 1903.

Mansfield Memorial Museum is home to Elektro, a once-famous robot built by Westinghouse at its Mansfield factory in 1937. The company had started designing robotic protypes in 1924. It created Televox in 1927, Katrina van Televox in 1930, Built-in-Watchman in 1931 and Willie Vocalite in 1932. For a machine that was fabricated using nothing but analog technology, Elektro had a remarkable range of capabilities. Its internal gears allowed it to walk, and although it did so at a turtle's pace, this is still an extraordinary feat, as, even today, makers of bipedal robots have trouble getting their creations to do this unaided due to balance issues.

Elektro moved its mouth while speaking and was able to interact with its surroundings because it could see colors using photoelectric cells. It could even smoke a cigarette. It was completely voice controlled and could speak seven hundred words. It stood seven feet, six inches tall and weighed 260 pounds (this not counting its external sixty-pound "brain" located backstage). Its first public appearance occurred on April 21, 1939, in front of a crowd in Mansfield. There, it interrupted Westinghouse's president with its first words: "Quiet, please. I'm doing the talking." It did the same thing to a presenter during its debut at the World's Fair in New York City later that year.

As cutting edge as Elektro was, it was just one in a long line of analog automatons throughout history, most of which weren't called robots—not because they didn't fit that description, but because the word hadn't yet entered the English lexicon. It was coined by Slavic writer Karel Čapek in his 1921 play, *Rossum's Universal Robots*, a story inspired by the Jewish myth of the golem, the mindless servant created by a Kabbalist.

One of the most sophisticated analog automatons ever created was designed by Jacques de Vaucanson in the eighteenth century. He drew up the design for what he called the Flute Player while sick in his Paris bed. His flute-playing wooden figure was painted white to look like marble and stood five feet, five inches tall atop a four-and-a-half-foot-tall pedestal. A sophisticated clockwork system, complete with a metal tongue and complemented by a bellows, gave it the ability to play the flute in tune.

Debuting on February 11, 1738, at the Hôtel de Longueville, it was an instant success, despite the entrance fee of three livres, about one week's wage for a manual laborer. When attendance waned the next year, Vaucanson added a figure that played a pipe and drum as well as a mechanical duck. The latter, built to actual size, ate food in a realistic way, then digested and excreted it. It was able to drink water, quack, walk and flex its neck. In one wing alone, it had over four hundred parts.

In 1940, the robot dog Sparko debuted alongside Elektro in New York. Westinghouse made thirteen robots of different types, including a female version of Elektro, the idea being that the company would develop a line of them for sale to the general public. This never happened. In 1950 and 1951, Westinghouse employee Frank Ruth drove Elektro around the country in an orange truck called the Elektromobile to visit county and state fairs in the summer and indoor venues, including department stores, in the winter. Next, Elektro became an exhibit in the House of Tomorrow at the Pacific Ocean Park in Santa Monica, California. In 1960, it appeared in the truly awful comedy *Sex Kittens Go to College*. For this movie, it was painted silver, and its torso was covered by a sleeveless sweater. Elektro's character was named Thinko.

In the 1970s, Elektro's head was removed and given to a retiring Westinghouse engineer, Harold Gorsuch. Its body was auctioned off. John Weeks eventually came into possession of the head after his brother moved into Gorsuch's house and found it in the basement. John's son Jack first encountered the head at the age of eight. He decided to reunite the head with the rest of its body. In 1990, Mansfield's Westinghouse plant closed, and Weeks loaned the head for the farewell party. A photograph of it appeared in a newspaper, and soon after, a fellow named John McDevitt contacted Weeks and said he had acquired the body when he bought the Elektromobile at an auction in the 1980s.

Weeks quickly headed to see what McDevitt had and was disappointed to find that the latter possessed two crates: one containing a silver torso and the other robotic limbs. Unaware of Elektro's color change—he had expected to see gold—Weeks wasn't sure this was what he had long sought after, and in any case, McDevitt wanted too much money for it. In 2004, a local museum asked Weeks if it could borrow the head, prompting him to return to McDevitt to take another look at the robotic torso he'd seen. McDevitt had died a few years earlier, but his brother-in-law arranged for Weeks to see the body. By then, some of the silver paint had peeled off, revealing the gold beneath.

Weeks bought Elektro's remains for $500 and began the arduous restoration process, eventually putting it on display in the Mansfield Memorial Museum. Now stationary—only its arms and head can move—Elektro also lacks a voice, as that portion of the mechanism has been lost. Elektro can be found on display in the museum so long as Weeks is alive. Upon his death, it is to be donated to the Henry Ford Museum in Dearborn, Michigan.

18

STARK COUNTY

The Underground Railroad

W ere it not for the efforts of Irene McLain Wales, Spring Hill House in Massillon would be just another old house in an upscale neighborhood alongside other large homes. Fortunately, Wales spent her life researching the history of the house in which she lived, and after she died, it became a museum based on her work. Though altered to accommodate modern updates, such as central heating and indoor plumbing, the house was put in the National Register of Historic Places in in 1972. Once a stop on the Underground Railroad, it was built by Thomas Rotch, a member of the Religious Society of Friends, or the Quakers.

Born in 1767, he worked for his family's whaling and shipping company based out of New Bedford and Nantucket, Massachusetts. Two of its ships were involved with the Boston Tea Party. On June 6, 1790, Rotch married Charity Rodman, a fellow Quaker and native of Newport, Rhode Island, who had been born there in 1765. Her father was a sea captain who died in Honduras when she was an infant. The Rotches moved to New Bedford and then, around 1801, relocated to Hartford, Connecticut, where Thomas became a farmer and wool manufacturer.

When Charity's doctor recommended she move to a milder climate, she and her husband decided on Ohio as their new home because it was a free state. (It's debatable whether or not Ohio winters are less brutal than those of New England.) The idea was to start a wool manufacturer, and to that end, they needed good pastureland and a water source to power the factory.

Spring Hill Historic Home was once a stop on the Underground Railroad. *Photograph taken by the author.*

These conditions were met along the Sippo Creek. Thomas established the settlement of Kendal, which was later absorbed by nearby Massillon. Returning home to settle affairs there, the Rotches returned in a carriage to their new property, along with four hundred Merino sheep and six men, a journey that took two months.

On the far side of Spring Hill's basement is a back stairway that was once used by servants. The stairs are exceedingly narrow and steep, making one believe that anyone climbing them regularly had to be part mountain goat. It's said the Rotches used these stairs to move fugitive enslaved people between floors to keep them out of sight. Enslaved people were also hidden in the sugar closet, which, ironically, contained no such substance—at least not when the Rotches lived in the house. Because sugarcane came primarily from Caribbean plantations, the Rotches refused to purchase it and instead used alternative sweeteners, like honey and maple sugar.

In 1776, the Quakers banned its members from possessing chattel enslaved people altogether. This opposition started not because the institution itself was seen as immoral but because the excessive profits made from slave trading were seen as immoral. In time, Quakers came to the conclusion that chattel slavery was a morally repugnant, evil institution, and by the late eighteenth century, many had started helping escaped enslaved people gain their freedom. One of the earliest mentions of this came in the 1780s from a bitter George Washington, who complained that the Quakers were helping his enslaved people escape.

The back stairs at Spring Hill Historic Home are said to have been used to move slaves covertly. *Photograph taken by the author.*

Their effort was the precursor to the Underground Railroad, whose founders didn't give it that name. The appellation first appeared around 1831 and was supposedly coined by a Kentucky slave owner who, angry at losing his $1,000 worth of "property," blamed the abolitionists, sarcastically remarking that they must run an underground railroad into which enslaved people vanished. Although no such infrastructure ever existed, the Underground Railroad did adopt the language of the railway. Those who helped move enslaved people became known as conductors, and the places where they hid them were called stations. Most conductors worked in the dark of night, with the average distance traveled each night being between six and twelve miles.

There are many myths about the Underground Railroad. Codes weren't woven into quilts because that would've been too time consuming to be effective. Stations didn't put out lanterns or candles as signals to escapees. One source said that there is no evidence that tunnels, secret or otherwise, were used, but this isn't the case. The house of Joseph Morris in Marion, Ohio, for example, had a secret room in the basement from which two tunnels could be accessed: one that took a person to the corn crib and another that took them to a barn.

One of the Underground Railroad's most important members was William Still. His father, Levin Steel, had purchased his freedom and changed his name to Still thereafter. His mother, Charity, whose enslaved name was Cidney, escaped from her bondage, leaving two of her four children behind. Born near Medford, New Jersey, William was denied a formal education, so he taught himself to read and write. In 1847, he married Letitia George, and in the same year, he was hired as a clerk by the Pennsylvania Society for the Abolition of Slavery at its Philadelphia headquarters.

William Still, from *The Underground Railroad from Slavery to Freedom*, by Wilbur Henry Sieber. *Courtesy of Wikipedia.*

The passage of the Fugitive Slave Act of 1850 caused Still's employer to revive its Vigilance Committee, which was dedicated to helping fugitive enslaved people escape. Still became its chairman; he helped many enslaved people escape, possibly as many as eight hundred. This number included his half-brother, Peter, who had been left behind when his mother escaped. After John Brown's failed attack on Harpers Ferry, several of Brown's accomplices stayed with Still for a brief time. Still kept detailed records of all those he and his compatriots helped, and he used that as the basis of his 1872 book, *The Underground Railroad*. He is considered by some as the father of the Underground Railroad.

It's estimated that by 1850, the number of escaped enslaved people given aid by the Underground Railroad was 100,000. Ohio had around 1,200 successful escapes each year, making it one of the most active states in the Underground Railroad. This was mainly due to Ohio's geography. Bordering two slave states, escapees who made it to Ohio cities along the shore of Lake Erie, such as Sandusky, Lorain, Cleveland and Painesville, could take a boat into nearby Canada, where slavery was completely banned. At least twenty routes passed through the state, purposely splintering off into many branches (another railroad term) to make it hard for slave catchers to follow escapees. It is estimated that Ohio had 1,543 members of the Underground Railroad, at least 100 of them were Black, compared to the 1,670 Black operators in all other states combined. In total, between 40,000 and 50,000 enslaved people escaped to freedom via Ohio, costing slave owners somewhere in the vicinity of $30 million.

Slave catchers once paid Spring Hill a visit. In the spring of 1820, a runaway and her two children came to Spring Hill, asking for help. Rotch hid them away for the night in the Spring Hill House. The next morning, two men on horseback rode up to the door to ask if Thomas Rotch lived in the house. Rotch answered that he did. The men identified themselves as slave hunters, one of whom knew the routes of the Underground Railroad because he had previously helped enslaved people escape along it. The other man identified himself as de Camp.

De Camp said he knew Rotch had hidden away the fugitives for whom he had a warrant giving him the authority to seize them. Rotch dared the slave catchers to find them and then said they would have trouble taking them if they did. By that point, several of Rotch's farmhands had arrived and given the horsemen menacing look. Intimidated, they departed. It seems unlikely that a Quaker would condone even the hint of violence, considering that religion's commitment to pacifism, but it's possible that Rotch felt it was

A BOLD STROKE FOR FREEDOM.

Black people pointing guns at slave catchers. *Courtesy of the Library of Congress.*

justified—or he was one of those Quakers who was less averse to the use of violence than some of his brethren. The source from which this story comes says de Camp was well known, yet the author of this book was unable to find a hint of his existence elsewhere in the historical record, so it's possible the entire story is apocryphal.

In September 1823, Thomas died while at the Quakers' yearly meeting in Mount Pleasant. The Rotches never had children. Charity passed on August 6, 1824. Her will set aside $20,000 to establish a school in which indigent children and orphans were to be taken care of and educated. Called the Charity Rotch School of Kendal and built on the Rotch's farm, it cost $5,000 to construct and opened in 1829. It operated until 1906, by which time, over five hundred children had attended the school. It admitted ten-year-old children for a four-year term. The boys learned farming, and the girls learned domestic work.

After Charity's death, one of the men who had accompanied the couple to Ohio and worked for Thomas, Alvis Wales, took possession of the house, along with 185 acres of farmland. He continued running his former employer's businesses. His son Alvin II became a lawyer in Massillon and an important civil leader. The house stayed in the family's possession until it became a museum. Local folklore says that William Henry Harrison slept overnight at the Spring Hill House during his 1840 presidential campaign, but it is more likely that he stayed in a local hotel.

19

SUMMIT COUNTY

Canals, Quarries and Paper Mills: Cuyahoga Valley and the Village of Peninsula

P eninsula was settled and named in 1837. Hermon Bronson, a Waterbury, Connecticut native who had come Ohio, arranged for its survey. He built its first grist and sawmills and got the Ohio and Erie Canal to pass through. Lock no. 29 was built here. Peninsula is now within the borders of the Cuyahoga Valley National Park, and because of this isolation, all of the village's water comes from wells, and everyone has their own septic tanks for lack of a sewer system. Peninsula rarely constructs new buildings and houses—so much so that the Peninsula Area Chamber of Commerce, in association with the Peninsula Library & Historical Society, has produced an excellent four-page guide, *Peninsula Village Architectural Tour*, which lists twenty historic buildings a person can see while on a walking tour. Several of these buildings are made of sandstone that came from the now-defunct quarries dotting the area.

On one of the exterior walls of the Peninsula Library & Historical Society, you can see an abstract mural by artist Honoré Guilbeau Cooke, in which the Cuyahoga River looks suspiciously snake-like. This represents an event that occurred in 1944. A few days after D-Day, two pythons supposedly escaped from the Cole Bros. Circus, which denied this. One python was found dead near Doylestown, and the other slithered about, scaring people. The trouble with the story is that it was first reported by Robert Bordner, a writer for the *Cleveland Press* who was known for perpetrating hoaxes.

In an article he wrote for the *Atlantic Monthly*, not known for publishing hokum, Bordner outlined the story in full, and he swore it was all true. The first person to see the python was Clarence Mitchell on June 8. He saw it while hoeing his cornfield near the abandoned Ohio and Erie Canal. For two the days prior, Mitchell's dogs had been nervous and refused to go near this spot. Mitchell watched the python, which he estimated to be between fifteen and eighteen feet long, slide into the Cuyahoga River, swim across and then slither up the other side. Another man also saw the snake.

Paul and John Szalay, while digging a ditch, saw the snake at Old Cassidy's Bottom ten days later (this was about two miles north of Mitchell's home). They hastily departed. Swearing the snake had left a track as wide as a car tire, the men sent word of the sighting to Mayor John Ritch. He, in turn, gathered the police chief, Art Huey, and his two assistant chiefs, Dale Hall and Dud Watson, to investigate. They concurred that "a mighty big snake" had made that track.

Two days later, Mrs. Roy Vaughn called the fire department in the morning to report that she had seen the reptile trying to go through a wire fence. Having just eaten, its expanded middle prevented it from succeeding in its effort. Undaunted, it climbed up and over this barrier, leaving behind a trail of destruction. It was probably responsible for a missing chicken. By measuring the distance between the fence and where Mrs. Vaughn said it had stretched to, Chief Huey determined that the snake was nineteen feet long.

Fletcher Reynolds from the Cleveland Zoo insisted the snake would not harm anyone so long as they stayed ten feet away. It could certainly strangle a person if it wrapped itself around them. He asked that no one scare it and to instead contact him. Mayor Ritch had other ideas. He declared a hunt for the snake on Sunday, June 25.

Locals put out traps. One person tried to lure it out using music. Others advocated grabbing it by the tail. The police broke people up into posses that swelled in number as people got out of church. The mayor, alarmed at the assorted weapons carried by the citizens, forbade all but law enforcement and posse leaders from possessing them for the hunt.

When the town hall siren erupted in three extended blasts, the hunt was on. Someone had called to report that their prey had been seen on author Fred Kelly's property to the east. The call had been a hoax. An hour later, the chase was called off, though smaller groups kept looking. Two days later, a posse was called to investigate a sighting along the river, near the unincorporated village of Boston Mills, but it found nothing.

A former resident of Peninsula who lived in Idaho Falls, Idaho, returned to his hometown to hunt the beast since he'd already made a hobby of catching rattlesnakes and selling their venom in Michigan, where it was made into antivenom for horses. He carried nothing more than a blanket, the idea being that when the snake struck it, he'd wrap it up. He went home empty-handed. No one ever caught the snake or found its carcass.

Whether the story is true is hard to say. It's certainly plausible, but then again, so are the best hoaxes. In favor of it being true, counterintuitively, is that fact that the snake was never caught. Pythons are not easy to find. Burmese pythons, the invasive species that is currently devastating Florida's ecology, are notoriously difficult to see due to their natural camouflage, which is made all the more effective by the fact that they stay stationary for long periods, waiting for prey. When Florida hosted the Python Challenge from January 12 to February 12, 2013, in which the idea was to hunt the pythons down to reduce their numbers, the almost 3,800 participants from thirty-eight states who registered for the hunt found a mere sixty-eight snakes, though it's true that most of them were not experienced snake hunters.

Peninsula began as one of the settlements along the Ohio and Erie Canal that once stretched from Cleveland down to the Ohio River at Portsmouth. The State of Ohio initially tried to finance the canal using a lottery, but few tickets were sold, forcing the state to instead rely on loans. Ground was broken for the canal on July 4, 1825, near Newark. Most of the backbreaking labor to dig the canal was done primarily by Irish immigrants who worked from sunup to sundown for a grand total of thirty cents a day—plus some whiskey.

Construction began at one of the canal's highest points, Portage Summit, near Akron, and from there, it went to Cleveland. This section was opened on June 27, 1827, with the launching of three boats that were not allowed to go faster than four miles per hour. The entire canal was completed in 1832. In the canal's early days, canal boats carried most of their cargo in bales, baskets or barrels.

These early vessels, called line boats, were usually eighty feet long, fourteen feet wide and between four feet and four and a half feet deep, with a draft of about three feet. They could carry a maximum of forty-five tons. They hauled both passengers and cargo. One of earliest industries in both Peninsula and nearby Boston Mills was canal boat building. The two yards produced more canal boats than any other yard along the canal's route—though that wasn't exactly a large number. During its peak year, 1862, the Peninsula yard built just thirty-two boats, and by the early 1870s, the industry had died out.

The traffic through the canal was heavily regulated, and those without permits to operate were not allowed on the canal. Paperwork was necessary

Erie and Ohio Canal's Lock 29. *Courtesy of the Library of Congress.*

for all boats loading and unloading so that the correct tolls could be accessed. Boat operators didn't necessarily follow these rules. Some boats had hidden compartments. One traveled between Cleveland and Akron without stopping at either toll station; therefore, it traveled down the canal without paying. This didn't mean the boat's owner operated for free. He either had to have his own tow animals or rent them—this was the costliest part of canal operations. In 1860, a firm in Chillicothe started making steam engines for canal boats, a power source that ultimately replaced draft animals.

By 1850, the canal was in dire need of repair and had lost much of its business to the railroads. The Ohio General Assembly considered selling the entire system, but in 1855, it instead gave private companies five-year contracts to carry out the repair and maintenance work. These firms took the money but did little else, leaving parts of the canal system impassable. Though it had never been a big money maker, the canal had served a greater purpose. It transformed Ohio from a backwater frontier to an agricultural powerhouse. The thirty-seven counties through which the canal traveled saw a dramatic 1,400 percent rise in real estate prices between 1826 and 1859.

Parts of the Ohio and Erie Canal continued to operate until 1913, when a massive flood wrecked it for good. Caused by a mixture of melting snow and rain, this flood rampaged through Ohio and other parts of the United States, causing extensive damage. In the Cuyahoga Valley, virtually no factory escaped damage, forcing about twenty thousand workers into unemployment for at least a week. In Akron, some of the Ohio and Erie Canal's locks were dynamited to reduce the flooding. A dam built by the Cleveland-Akron Bag Company Factory at Boston Mills was blown up on March 27, lowering water level by ten inches.

Peninsula's Main Street Bridge, which crossed the Cuyahoga River and the Ohio and Erie Canal, was wiped out, leaving the town divided by water. Lock no. 29 and a connecting aqueduct were also lost, as was the Broughton Store. Tracks at the Cleveland & Mahoning Valley Railroad Depot were in ruins, and some tracks near Brecksville were twisted like corkscrews. It took a week before the postal service was restored. Provisions became scarce.

After the flood, parts of the canal were repurposed to provide water to the area's industries. Other sections were still used for boat traffic. Ohio decommissioned the last navigable section in July 1929. The canal's destruction had little fiscal impact on the Cuyahoga Valley in general or Peninsula in particular because other industries had already replaced it. Quarrying boomed when the railroad came to Peninsula because it was much easier to transport stone via train than on the canal.

Many of the stones that were used to build the Ohio and Erie Canal's locks came from the valley's Deep Lock Quarry, which also produced grindstones, millstones, pulp stones and stones for buildings. It closed in 1917. Keeping track of the various quarrying companies that operated there is not for the faint of heart. Leases were sold, and ownerships frequently changed. The earliest known quarrying was carried out on land owned by Hermon Bronson, the same man who had surveyed the land on which Peninsula was founded. He sold his stone for use in the construction of the Ohio and Erie Canal's lock no. 31.

At this time, stone was cut by making a slot on either side with a pick, then inserting wedges into these slots to cause a piece to break away. Over the years, new technologies made rock quarrying more efficient and, in some cases, easier. Cutting out rock leaves behind rubble called overburden that, for much of the nineteenth century, was hauled out of the Cuyahoga Valley's quarries by horse-drawn carts. In 1890, a small locomotive named *Dinky* was put into the South Quarry to replace animal power. Though it

This bridge being ripped away during the 1913 flood is located in Cleveland. *Courtesy of the Library of Congress.*

went just a few miles per hour, it could pull far more rock than any team of animals. It was also safer because quarries produce a lot of noises that spook horses—in this state of mind, horses are known to trample people to death. Yet, on the *Dinky*'s first day of operation, it backed up into a guy wire, causing a derrick to fall that injured one worker and killed two others, John Wagner and John Mullins. Engines such as this one were placed on portable tracks akin to a child's railroad set, this being necessary because quarries were always deepening and widening.

Quarrying is, even today, a dangerous venture for those involved. Crushed limbs—if not bodies—were common. Slippery wet stones caused falls. The most dangerous piece of equipment was the derrick, as demonstrated by the accident with the *Dinky*. Stone dust presented its own danger, though it takes its time to do its work. It can damage a quarryman's lungs, causing the disease pneumonoultramicroscopicsilicovolcanoconiosis, which is quite a mouthful and not a word someone with breathing issues wants to say out loud. These days, quarries have a variety of safety measures to reduce the amount of dust in the air, including spraying everything down.

South Quarry, Cuyahoga Valley's last quarry to shut down, did so in 1917. By this time, cement had greatly reduced need for sandstone in most construction projects. Fortunately, the paper mill industry had arrived to offer alternative employment. The valley was perfect for papermaking because it had an abundance of the two prime ingredients necessary for its creation: water and lumber. The first paper mills along the Cuyahoga River were opened in 1899.

One of these paper mills was founded by Charles Jaite in 1905. As a boy, he had emigrated from Germany, and in his teenage years, he had worked in the paper-making business in Cleveland. He located his mill near both the Ohio and Erie Canal and Cleveland Terminal & Valley Railroad to make shipping his products easy. His mill employed farmers who needed extra money, as well as a large number of immigrants (in 1918, this amounted to around 250 immigrants).

In 1906, Jaite built five two-story buildings to house his employees, and in 1917, he expanded that with the construction of four single-family homes along Vaughn Road. A small town grew up around the mill that included a post office, railroad depot and a general store. Jaite paid his workers in hard cash, not scrip like so many others who ran company towns. His workers were also not forced to live in the housing he provided. Even in 1933, during the worst year of the Great Depression, his mill continued to run twenty-four hours a day, seven days a week.

Jaite Paper Mill. *Courtesy of the Library of Congress.*

It made bread sacks and bags for fertilizer, and its Blue Line paper was used for flour packaging and cement bags. The Jaite family sold the mill in 1951, and after going through several owners, the National Park Service bought its building in 1975. Unlike the other paper mills that were operating along the Cuyahoga River, this mill's water came from artesian wells, allowing it to outlast the others that were forced to close when the river's polluted water made it impossible to continue operations. The mill building is currently the Cuyahoga Valley National Park's headquarters.

The Cleveland-Akron Bag Company, which made roofing paper and flour sacks, tried to cope with river pollution by damming the Spring Creek. Located in Boston Mills, it also owned the Boston General Store, which was run for many years by Chester and Julia Zielenski. The mill closed in 1923, and two years later, the couple bought the store outright. In 1928, the abandoned mill was purchased by the Union Trust, but the company offered no reprieve. The mill was torn down in 1932.

20

TRUMBULL COUNTY

The Birthplace of Packard Motor

Anyone with a cursory knowledge of the Packard Motor Company will probably associate it with Detroit. But its origins lie in the Trumbull County city of Warren. James Packard and his old brother, William, cofounded the company. The former was born on November 5, 1863, and the latter was born on November 3, 1861. William was the businessman, and James was the mechanic. There's no doubt that their motivation to start businesses together was inspired by their entrepreneurial father, who owned several successful businesses in Warren. William graduated from Ohio State University. James attended Leigh University in Bethlehem, Pennsylvania, where he graduated in 1884 with a degree in mechanical engineering. His first job was in New York City at the Sawyer-Man Electric Company, which made incandescent lightbulbs; it was later absorbed by Westinghouse.

After six years of learning about the electrical industry, James moved back to Warren in 1890. That year, he, along with his brother and some New York investors, founded the Packard Electric Company. This company would manufacture transformers and a lamp that James had patented the year before. The factory was ready in September, and the company was started with ten employees. The New York investors started a second company, the New York and Ohio Company, which bought Packard Electric's products and sold them all over the United States. William served as its salesman, going around the country marketing its products to large cities and privately owned lighting companies.

James had an interest in the newfangled automobiles that were starting to take to the roads, though the first self-powered vehicle he bought was a motor-powered tricycle built by the French company De Dion-Bouton. Started as a manufacturer of railcars, De Dion-Bouton later moved on to building high-quality automobiles, which became its primary product until the Great Depression brought about its demise. Tricycles were just a sideline, though the oldest known motorbike that is still capable of running is an 1887 tricycle the company made. James wasn't impressed with his.

James hired Edward P. Cowles in 1896 to build him a motor wagon, but after two years of work, it came to nothing. James then looked at a car designed by Youngstown physician Carlos Booth. Always in a hurry, Booth built his car not because he had a vision of the future of what transportation would be like or a desire to sell his invention; rather, he despised horses. In 1891, a spooked horse that was pulling a carriage carrying his father-in-law and two sisters-in-law ran in front of freight train, killing all but his younger sister-in-law, Ella. In 1895, a horse pulling the buggy in which he and his wife rode was spooked and ran into traffic, resulting in an accident that put his wife in the hospital and on the danger list.

In the same month of the latter accident, James read about the Bordeaux-Paris Race and thought that an automobile would be better than a horse for making house calls. With no automobiles available domestically that he knew of, James drafted a rough design for one and sent it to W. Lee Crouch of the Pierce-Crouch Engine Company in New Brighton, Pennsylvania, to build the engine. He turned to the Fredonia Manufacturing Company in Youngstown to make the body.

The new car weighed 1,040 pounds and was propelled by a one-cylinder engine capable of taking it up to sixteen miles per hour. In 1886, Booth entered his car into a race sponsored by the magazine *Cosmopolitan* that went from City Hall in New York City to Irvington-on-Hudson and back, a total of fifty-two miles. Booth made it to Irvington-on-Hudson but broke down on his return. A sore loser, he was incensed that he had won nothing, considering other cars hadn't even gotten past the starting line. The $3,000 prize went to a car that had initially broken down and then later finished the race; Boothe refused to race again.

He converted his car's body to that of an enclosed one so that he could use it in all types weather, possibly making his the first car of this type in America. Modifications to the engine got the vehicle up to twenty and twenty-five miles per hour. But the car frightened horses so much that Booth found it difficult to drive anywhere because he had to keep stopping to move horses out of his way. Sick of this, he sold his car in 1897 and went back to a horse and buggy. When cars became more common, he returned to this mode of transportation.

In 1898, James traveled to Cleveland and bought a car from Winton Motor Carriage Company. Winton Motor's founder, Alexander Winton, was born in Grangemouth, Scotland, on June 20, 1860. His father made farm equipment. As a young man, Winton apprenticed at the shipyards on the River Clyde, and after that, he came to the United States, where he eventually settled in Cleveland. While working as the plant superintendent at Phoenix Iron Works, which made furnaces, Winton started a bicycle repair business that expanded into manufacturing them in 1891. During the bicycle craze of the 1890s, his shop built between five thousand and six thousand of these machines.

Winton was probably the first bicycle maker in Cleveland to dabble in the manufacturing of cars. Between 1893 and 1895, he experimented with putting engines on bicycles. He made his first four-wheel gasoline-powered vehicle in 1896 and incorporated his auto company the next year. Wanting to show what one of his vehicles could do, on July 28, 1897, Winton set out in a single seat two-cylinder car that weighed 1,800 pounds and was powered by an internal combustion engine that used cleaning fluid bought from hardware stores along the way as fuel. It took two days for him to reach New York City. From there, he drove to and through Syracuse, Utica and Albany.

Aside from drumming up publicity, which Winton felt was insufficient, he had also undertaken the venture to test the endurance of his engine and his car's ability to travel over roads, which he characterized as "simply outrageous." He estimated the entire trip was eight hundred miles long. Two years later, he did it again, this time paying professional journalist Charles B. Shanks, a reporter for the *Cleveland Plain Dealer*, to accompany him and publicize the effort. Afterward, Shanks became Winton's advertising manager.

Winton often promoted his cars by racing them, something many early carmakers did. On October 10, 1901, he raced an upstart automaker named Henry Ford at Grosse Pointe Racetrack in Detroit. Ford's win helped launch his career. Later that year, Winton became a dirt track champion. In 1903, he set a speed record of sixty-eight miles per hour at Daytona Beach, Florida. In 1905, he built an eight-cylinder racecar that millionaire James Gordon Bennett drove at the race in Ireland he founded called the Gordon Bennett Cup. Bennett lost, claiming someone had put candle wax in his gas tank not to sabotage him but to "keep way the devils," as cars were seen as demonic in that era.

Although Winton Motor was quite successful during its early years, Winton, a stubborn and cantankerous man, failed to realize that the only way his company could survive after the introduction of the Model T was to embrace mass production and build a low-cost competing vehicle. He didn't drop "Carriage" from his company's name until 1914, and it wasn't until that year that he moved his cars' steering apparatus from the right to the left. The electric starter was finally introduced in 1915, only because of dealer demand. Instead of building a car for the masses, Winton stopped making cars altogether in 1924 and got into fabricating diesel marine engines.

The Winton car that James Packard had bought didn't make it all the way to Warren, forcing Packard to hire a team of horses to bring it the rest of the way. Winton sent his foreman, William Hatcher, to Warren to repair the vehicle. It took him two days to get it running. It never ran well, and James repeatedly returned to Cleveland for repairs. It was during his last visit, on June 10, 1899, that Winton supposedly told him that if he was so clever with his suggestions for improvements, perhaps he should build a car of his own.

So, that's what Packard did. Winton's biggest investor, George Weiss, decided to put his money toward Packard. Packard hired Hatcher away from Winton to help build and design car. Hatcher had an eighth-grade education and was largely self-taught, which was not unusual in those days. He was hired on to build the prototype for $100.00 a week. Hatcher created most of the new car's plans. Space for him was set aside in the New York and Ohio factory. James collaborated closely, and the two men jointly took out six patents for their work. The prototype made its first trip onto the streets of Warren on November 6, 1899. The new car company was incorporated in 1900 as the Ohio Automobile Company. It employed seventeen workers who were paid $0.20 an hour, about $6.26 in 2021.

The very first Packard produced, the Model A, had no serial number; only five were ever built. Although the steering wheel had been introduced by Alfred Vacheron in 1894, at this point, it hadn't been universally adapted, so the Model A had a tiller. The bodies for the Model A and B were built by carriage makers Morgan and Williams. The Packard brothers kept the very first Model A and eventually donated it to Lehigh University, where it can still be seen today. The first car the company sold went to Weiss on April 13, 1900.

The Model B was the first production vehicle. At a glance, the Models A and B look nearly identical, but many mechanical changes and improvements were made with the second-generation car. One difference was that the

Packard Model C, National Packard Museum. *Photograph taken by the author.*

Model A had a lever to control acceleration, and the Model B had a pedal. The delivery of the first Model B was reported by the *Warren Daily Chronicle* on April 13, 1900. The car on display in Warren's National Packard Museum was the tenth built. It was sold to George Blackmore, a businessman from Painesville. As an added service, Packard's head machinist, Henry Schryver, accompanied Blackmore on the trip home to teach him to drive and how to perform basic maintenance. Forty-nine Model Bs were built and cost $1,325, about $41,487 in 2021.

Next came the Model C, eighty-two of which were made. In appearance, it didn't differ much from the previous two models. An optional steering apparatus was on offer that could be tilted up to allow the driver to get into the seat. The horsepower increased from nine to twelve, and the shifter was set to an H pattern. Model Cs were bought by Hollis Honeywell and William Rockefeller at the debut National Auto Show in New York City, signifying that it was a luxury vehicle.

With 1901 came all sorts of significant Packard moments. The slogan "ask the man who owns one" debuted. With no auto ignition cable capable of handling the power needed for the car's sparkplug, Packard Electric developed one called the Packard Lac-Kard Cable. Packard machinists went on strike, demanding higher wages and a fifty-two-hour week. Henry Bourne Joy of Detroit invested in the company because he liked his Packard so much, particularly its ability to start reliably. Joy's involvement in the company would radically alter its future.

In 1902, Joy increased his investment and therefore had a greater say in the company's operation and direction. In that same year,

Henry Bourne Joy. *Courtesy of the Library of Congress.*

Weiss resigned as vice-president and director of the company. The company built a twelve-thousand-square-foot two-story factory; hired French racecar driver Charles Smidt to improve the design of future cars and add more complexity to them; and renamed itself the Packard Motor Company. By then, it needed to refinance and raise capital for further expansion, so Joy took charge of this. A total of 2,500 shares were sold at one hundred dollars apiece, mostly to Detroit investors, allowing them to effectively take control of the company on October 13, 1902, with Joy as its head.

Joy was born on November 23, 1865, to a wealthy railroad family. Like many industrial leaders of his day, Joy had his hand in many ventures at the same time. In addition to running Packard, he helped found the Lincoln Highway project, the nation's first coast-to-coast highway that was meant to promote auto travel, and occupied himself with hobbies that included skeet shooting (he once set a world record, hitting 157 clay pigeons consecutively), shortwave broadcasting, aviation and running a bird sanctuary.

At the outbreak of World War I, Joy advocated for better defense preparedness and conscription and railed against German submarine warfare. Unlike many advocates of war readiness, when the United States entered the fight in 1917, he joined the army and served as a lieutenant colonel. He had previously served on the USS *Yosemite* during the Spanish-American War and had joined army troops in their futile pursuit of Pancho Villa in Mexico. A lifelong Republican, in 1929, he quit the Detroit Republican Club due to his party's continued embrace of Prohibition.

Despite the fact Packard had just built a new factory in Warren in 1902, Joy and those who controlled the company decided to move production to Detroit. A new facility opened there on October 10, 1903; it was filled with equipment and workers from the former premises. After losing control of the company, James stayed in Warren to pursue work at Packard Electric as well as the New York and Ohio Company. James Packard officially remained president of Packard Motors until 1909; he served as board chairman until 1912 and remained a board member until 1915. Despite his lack of input in the company's operations and direction, he kept his considerable amount of company stock.

Packard Electric continued to produce innovative electrical products. In 1933, the company became part of General Motors and took on the new name Delphi Packard Electric Systems, which exists today as Delphi Technologies. During World War II, it made harnesses for tanks, cables for airplanes and wires for trucks, armored cars and other military vehicles. Its motor was used in the remote-controlled antiaircraft guns found on American bombers.

21

TUSCARAWAS COUNTY

The Massacre at Gnadenhutten

To understand the founding of the village of Gnadenhutten, it's first necessary to travel to Europe and look at the origins of the religious group known as the Moravians. They trace their roots back to the mid-fifteenth-century teachings of John Hus. Their founding preceded the Reformation, which was sparked when Martin Luther wrote his Ninety-Five Theses, which he didn't nail to any doors. Hus was born in 1369, only eighteen years after the Black Death completed its deadly rampage through Europe. In adulthood, Hus was a professor of philosophy as well as a rector at the University of Prague. He preached in Bethlehem Chapel, where he railed against the Roman Catholic Church's hierarchy and clergy. Not keen on such dissent, the Catholic Church tried him for heresy at the Council of Constance. Found guilty, he was burned at the stake on July 6, 1415.

He inspired the creation of a church that called itself the Unitas Fratrum (Unity of Brethren). Founded by Gregory the Patriarch in 1457 in the eastern Bohemian village of Kunvald, the Unitas Fratrum believed Christianity was defined by following what Christ taught, not a rigorous doctrine. By 1517, it had a minimum of 200,000 members who were spread across about four hundred parishes. The Thirty Years' War broke out between the Catholics and the Protestants. Raging from 1618 to 1648, it was the worst European religious conflict of its kind. One of its many battles led to the effective destruction of Moravian Church in 1620, when a Catholic force defeated Bohemian Protestants at the Battle of White Mountain.

In 1722, Count Nikolaus Ludwig von Zinzendorf resurrected the church on his estate in Saxony, where Moravians who were fleeing the religious wars had been allowed to establish the community of Herrnhut. They also started heading to North America. In 1735, the first Moravians to go to North America landed in the English colony of Georgia, although a war between Spain and Britain that broke out in 1739 derailed the new settlement. In 1741, more Moravians went to North America, this time to Pennsylvania, and from there, they spread to other colonies.

Accepting of all races and generally pacifistic, the Moravians' main tenet was missionary work. Early on in America, the religion gained many Native converts. One of the most successful Moravian missionaries was David Zeisberger, who was born in Zauchtenthal, Bohemia, on April 11, 1721. Educated in Herrnhut in Saxony, at the age of seventeen, he, along with his parents, arrived in Georgia to establish a new town. When that didn't work out, they moved north and ultimately settled in Bethlehem, Pennsylvania, which became the center of Moravian activities in North America. Zeisberger decided to become a missionary to North America's Native people, and to that end, he began learning their languages.

In March 1771, Delaware chief Netawatwees asked Zeisberger to visit his capital of Gekelmukpechunk (now Newcomerstown) to teach Christianity. The Delaware did not originate in Ohio, nor did they call themselves by that name. They were the Lenni Lenape, which meant "people of the standard" or "real people." This was often shortened to just Lenape. The English called them Delaware because when they first encountered the Lenape, they lived along the Delaware River, which was named in honor of Thomas West, Lord De La Warr, Virginia's second governor.

The Lenape were divided into the Wolf, Turkey and Turtle clans, the last of which Chief Netawatwees led. They were traditionally hunters and farmers, with a warrior class that used bows and arrows, tomahawks, spears and scalping knives to make war. They used shields made of hide for defense. European encroachment forced the Lenape to abandon their traditional lands, which encompassed modern Delaware, Pennsylvania, New Jersey and New York. Many Lenape resettled west in what is now Ohio.

The Grand Council in Gekelmukpechunk invited Christian Natives who were living in Pennsylvania's Wyoming Valley to Ohio, where there was an ongoing conflict on land that the Iroquois sold to the British, despite the fact they didn't have the right to do so. To accommodate these refugees, the Moravians in Bethlehem decided to establish missions in the Tuscarawas

Right: John Hus. *Courtesy of the Library of Congress.*

Below: John Sartain, *Zeisberger Preaching to the Indians*, 1864. *Courtesy of the Library of Congress.*

Valley. Zeisberger was put in charge of this venture, with John Heckewelder as his assistant.

Heckewelder had been born in 1743 in Bedford, England, where he got some of his early formal education. His German-speaking parents had come to Britain as religious refugees from Moravia. At the age of eleven, Heckewelder and his parents traveled to New York. When his parents left for the West Indies to do missionary work, Heckewelder stayed behind. He went to Bethlehem in the company of Bishop David Nitschmann to continue his education.

Attending Heckewelder's school were six young Natives who lived with their elders. His interaction with them prompted him to dedicate his life to working with these people. After becoming a missionary at the age of nineteen, Heckewelder accompanied Christian Frederick Post to a Native town in the Tuscarawas Valley, located approximately thirty miles south of where Akron now stands. There, he met Kogiesch Quanoheel, a Lenape chief of the Wolf clan known to the White settlers as Captain Pipe. Brothers Tamaqua (known to White settlers as King Beaver) and his brother Shingas "the Terrible," members of the Turkey clan, also lived here. Shingas was planning a war to push all of the white settlers east, to the other side of the Alleghany Mountains, with his ally Pontiac. When being unfriendly to Heckewelder didn't persuade the young man to go elsewhere, Shingas outright told him to leave, as his life was in danger. Heckewelder heeded this blunt warning and returned to Bethlehem with some English traders.

Zeisberger and Heckewelder were responsible for helping establish the villages of Schoenbrunn, Salem*, Litchtenau and Gnadenhutten. This last was first settled by forty Lenape, led by a Moravian elder (and Native) named Joshua, on October 9, 1772. The name Gnadenhutten translates to "huts of grace." For seven years, the village thrived because it had rich land for

This portrait of John Heckewelder is from his 1820 book, *A Narrative of the Mission of the United Brethren Among the Delaware and Mohegan Indians, from Its Commencement, in the Year 1740, to the Close of the Year 1808. Digitized by Google Books*.

---

* This is not the same Salem that was mentioned in chapter 4.

farming. The villagers also bred horses and raised livestock. The village's wealth was so great that its inhabitants could afford glass windows and basements. It was an integrated community, as evidenced by the birth of John Lewis Roth, a White baby born in Ohio on July 4, 1773. Some sources say he was the first White person born in Ohio, but there are others who also have claim to this title.

Before the outbreak of the American Revolution on April 19, 1775, the territory from which Ohio would one day be carved was forbidden to English settlers, though that didn't stop them from squatting. Since Ohio was a frontier, it wasn't until the summer of 1781 that the American Revolution's fighting reached the Moravians. Their villages stood along the most direct route between the American-controlled Fort Pitt and the British-held Detroit—a bad place to be for those who professed neutrality.

On August 12, 1781, a party of consisting of 140 Lenape, Wyandot, Shawnee, Chippewa and Tawa, carrying a British flag, arrived in Salem. Leading them was Wyandot chief Pomoacan, often called the half-king. Accompanying him but insisting that he had just happened to come along was a British agent named Captain Matthew Elliot, an American loyalist who was born in Ireland. Another who had joined the group was Captain Pipe. More warriors arrived the next day, increasing the group's total number to about 300.

Elliot went to Heckewelder's house to inform him that Pomoacan had something to say to all the Moravians' Native members, and he asked where they could all meet. Suspicious of their motives, Heckewelder pointed out that the Natives were all armed, indicating hostile intent. Elliot dismissed this out of hand. These people went everywhere armed. Heckewelder told Elliot to take his party to Gnadenhutten, where Moravian representatives from the other towns could parley with them. Before leaving, some of the warriors broke into and plundered Heckewelder's house.

The planned meeting occurred on August 20; there, Pomoacan warned that "two mighty and powerful spirits" were coming to swallow the Moravian settlements, the "spirits" representing the Americans and British. Pomoacan wanted to take them to safety under the protection of the British in Detroit. The missionaries thanked him for his concern and promised to give him an answer the next spring. This satisfied Pomoacan but not Elliot. The next day, Pomoacan announced that this wait was too long. On August 27, Zeisberger gave the chief a string of wampum and formally declined the offer. Pomoacan accepted, but his men didn't leave the village.

The unwanted visitors held a secret council in which they proposed murdering all the White missionaries and leveling the towns to entice the Native Moravians to come with them. Another general council was called on September 2 that was attended by Zeisberger, Heckewelder, William Edwards and Gotlob Senseman. The next day, as they were walking behind the gardens, Wyandot men seized them as prisoners and stripped them of their clothes. They were freed soon after.

Things came to a head on September 11. The Moravians were told to leave their villages with Pomoacan under escort by his warriors. They were taken to a place along the Sandusky River, where Upper Sandusky stands today. There, they were left to their own devices while their escorts, the Wyandot, continued to their home about ten miles away. The Moravians had no food or provisions with them, and the area had been hunted out. Industrious as always, they constructed temporary huts and tents as shelter while they worked to build new homes along the river. They called their place of exile Captives' Town.

Captain Pipe sent Chief Wenginund there to inform the White missionaries that the British commandant of Detroit wished to speak with them. Heckewelder thought this was due to the machinations of Captain Elliot, Captain Alexander M'kee and Simon Girty. For reasons of their own, they wanted the Moravians removed from the area, and to that end, they had sent Captain Pipe to Detroit to report that the missionaries were conspiring with the Americans. So, Zeisberger, Heckewelder, Senseman, Edwards and several Moravian Natives began their journey to Detroit.

They departed on October 25, and two days later, they arrived at Captain Pipe's camp, where many of his people were drunk. From there, they located Captain Elliot. Heckewelder wrote in his book *A Narrative of the Mission of the United Brethren Among the Delaware and Mohegan Indians* that he went to see Captain Elliot to ask him "if we could not be permitted to pursue our journey without Captain Pipe, as it was not likely that he would quit drinking for some time." Elliot said that this was out of the question. Heckewelder then "asked first, if he [Elliot] expected we would live to see the commandant at Detroit if we must wait for Pipe's becoming sufficiently sober, to go with us? And secondly, whether he believed that if the commandant could see the situation we were placed in here, as he now saw it, he would be indifferent, with regard to our safety?" Elliot thought about that and then replied that "he believed we might go on without Pipe, as we had some Indians with us who would protect us from the insults of warriors of other nations."

With that business settled, the journey was resumed. It was cold, and they didn't have decent clothes for the weather; upon reaching Lake Erie, they were stymied by bad roads, mires and swamps. Despite this hardship, they continued overland toward their destination. Just four miles from Detroit, they found themselves stranded at the River Rouge, as they lacked a way to cross. The next morning, two boats came down from Detroit and ferried them across the river. After arriving in Detroit on November 3, they hoped they would receive a hot breakfast. Guards refused to let them in until the commandant acquiesced. They were then brought to the house of an elderly French couple, Mr. and Mrs. Tybout, who took the missionaries in as guests.

It wasn't until November 9 that the commandant, Major Arent Schuyler de Peyster, finally saw them at his council house. Born in New York City on June 27, 1736, at the age of nineteen, de Peyster joined the Eighth Regiment in the British army and spent his career serving in North America, some of it under the command of his uncle Colonel Peter Schuyler. De Peyster took command of Detroit in October 1779.

He had a good relationship with Detroit's French population, and he treated his Native allies well, though he disliked some of the cruelties committed by them. According to *The City of Detroit, Michigan, 1701–1922*, de Peyster "urged them to bring in more prisoners and fewer scalps." He got into trouble when he was caught skimming rents that were due to the British Crown. When told to repay what he'd taken, he protested it would cause him a great financial burden—but to no avail. After the war, he settled in his wife's hometown of Dumfries, Scotland. A cultured man, in 1813, he published a book of poetry titled *Miscellanies by the Officer*.

In addition to the missionaries and the commandant, the meeting also included the British Indian agent Mr. Bawbee, along with two unidentified gentlemen and a number of Natives, including Captain Pipe. One war chief carried a stick hung with the scalps of Americans. De Peyster had the missionaries brought there because he'd heard they were communicating with rebels and plotting harm to Detroit. He was annoyed that the missionaries hadn't brought their entire families, but this was excused when it was pointed that out no one had told them to do so.

When de Peyster realized that the four White settlers before him were ministers, his attitude softened. It was the testimony of Captain Pipe of all people that exonerated the missionaries. He said it was his fault if they had done anything wrong and insisted that he never wanted any harm to come to them. He had been pressured to turn against them and now desired to speak truthfully. When asked what should be done with them, he answered that they should be able to go home. De Peyster asked the missionaries what their connection to the Continental Congress was. In a long-winded answer, they testified that it had never given them any instructions nor held any influence over them.

De Peyster acquitted them. On November 10 he told Zeisberger and Heckewelder and their fellow missionaries could go home. Without a penny to their name, he gave them provisions for their journey. They departed on November 14 and arrived back in Captives' Town on November 22. Food was, by then, becoming scarce, and this only became worse as late fall turned into winter. For a time, they managed to get some corn, but it soon ran out.

On February 9, 1782, the missionaries received permission from Detroit to return to their towns to gather up the unharvested corn. On March 1, Pomoacan summoned Zeisberger and Heckewelder to a meeting, where he informed them that de Peyster had ordered that all the White missionaries and their families return to Detroit. They asked that a boat take them there, as the overland route would have been too great a burden on the women and children; this was granted. They headed to Lower Sandusky (now Fremont) to board a boat bound for Detroit. Upon reaching the city on March 19, they received intelligence that de Peyster had summoned them because he feared for their safety. Four days later, the missionaries learned of a terrible massacre of the Moravian Natives, who had returned to their villages for food.

This terrible deed was done in the name of revenge in reaction to a mid-February attack carried out near Pittsburgh by a Lenape and Wyandot raiding party from Detroit, causing the deaths of Robert Wallace's wife and three children. On their way back to Detroit, the war party took several White prisoners and stopped briefly in Gnadenhutten for food. One of the prisoners, whose wife and child had been impaled by the Wyandot, escaped the next day. He likely made his way to Pittsburgh to raise the alarm and report what had happened.

Between 150 and 200 militiamen, commanded by Lieutenant Colonel David Williamson, set out for Gnadenhutten to exact revenge. The force probably departed without the knowledge of Fort Pitt's commander, Colonel John Gibson. Williamson's militia arrived at its target on March 8. About a mile out of town, it murdered and scalped Joseph Shabosh, despite his protestations that he was the son of a White man. Joseph's brother-in-law Jacob was working nearby. Knowing some of these men, he raised his hand to hail them when, to his astonishment, they shot one of his fellow Moravians who was passing in a canoe. The terrified Jacob made himself scarce.

The militia also murdered two Natives who were not associated with the Moravians. Shortly after these terrible deeds, the militia found most of the Moravians in the fields, working. Unaware of what had just happened, they had no reason to suspect any danger. The militia assured them that all was well and asked them to return to the village. The fact that the Moravians wore European-style clothes indicated that they'd had nothing to do with the war party that had sparked this punitive expedition, but those who were bent on vengeance didn't care.

John Martin and his son returned from an errand and were surprised to see that no one was in the field. Seeing White's men in the village, Martin sent his son there to see what was going on. He was told the militia planned to take them to safety. Martin then took his son to Salem to spread the news, and its citizens decided to head to Gnadenhutten. The sight of their dead comrade in the canoe alerted them to danger too late. They were taken prisoner and put with the others. Those in nearby Schoenbrunn had been warned and escaped.

In town, the militia bound all the Moravians, segregated them by sex and then imprisoned them in two houses. Not everyone in the militia was of the same mind about what to do with the prisoners. Some of them wanted to burn them alive; others preferred to scalp them. Still others wanted no part of this murder. In the end, mass murder was the course taken. One woman, Christiana, begged for the ladies' lives—but to no avail. The prisoners were given the chance to prepare themselves. Death would not be dealt until the next morning. Through the night, the prisoners prayed and sang.

In the morning, a cooper's mallet was used to slay them. Ninety-six were murdered. Some, if not all, were scalped. After completing their bloody work, the killers plundered the village, stripping it of everything of value. Before the massacre, they had forced the villagers to bring out their hidden valuables, including their honey. Beneath the stack of bodies laid a boy who had survived both blunt force trauma and scalping. After crawling out, he, along with Jacob, went to Captives' Town to report the massacre. Before heading back to Pittsburgh, the militia burned their victims' bodies and all the villagers' houses.

Williamson and his men returned home to Pennsylvania, but many of them, Williamson included, soon joined a militia of Pennsylvanians and Virginians, headed by Colonel William Crawford, with the mission of attacking the British-backed Lenape and Seneca living along the Sandusky River. Crawford, a Virginian born on June 11, 1732, had served under and became the friend of George Washington during their time in the colonial militia in 1755. After Crawford moved to Connellsville, Pennsylvania, Washington asked him to help him find some of the best land in the area to buy. As an occasional soldier, Crawford had gained fighting experience during Lord Dunmore's War, a land grab by Virginia's governor John Murray, Lord Dunmore, that captured territory controlled by the Mingo and Shawnee.

By the time Crawford and his approximately five hundred men reached the area near Upper Sandusky, rations had dwindled to the point at which it was necessary to turn back. On June 4, the British, alongside their Native allies, attacked, killing about fifty Americans at the Battle of Sandusky. The next day, a second skirmish, the Battle of the Olentangy, erupted, causing a general retreat. Crawford and several others stayed along the road to guard their rear. That night, Crawford and another man, surgeon's mate John Night, were captured.

The Natives who captured them wanted revenge for what had happened at Gnadenhutten. They stripped Crawford and Knight naked, tied them to a post and then "blacked" them, a repeated burning with a firebrand. The

The final burial place for the remains of those massacred at Gnadenhutten, Gnadenhutten Museum and Historic Site. *Photograph taken by the author.*

prisoners had to run a gauntlet of women, men and children, who beat them with sticks, clubs, fists and whatever else they had on hand. The next day, both men were blacked again.

A stake surrounded by red-hot coals was erected, and Crawford was made to walk over them barefoot. For about two hours, he was repeatedly poked with burning sticks. He begged Simon Girty, who stood there and watched, to shoot him, but he had no gun. Crawford's captors scalped him. He collapsed, and the women buried him in the coals; this last act of torture killed him. Facing the same fate, Knight whacked one of his captors on the head with a piece of firewood and escaped.

After Zeisberger's return from his second sojourn to Detroit, he never again set foot in Gnadenhutten. It was just too painful. In 1792, he led Moravian Natives to Canada and with them founded a new settlement at New Fairfield in Ontario. In 1813, this town was destroyed by an American incursion into Canada, led by William Henry Harrison, though it was rebuilt and survived until 1903. Zeisberger returned to Schoenbrunn. In 1792, founded Goshen near Cincinnati, where he died on November 17, 1808.

In 1798, Heckewelder returned to Gnadenhutten with the aim of rebuilding it. His first task was to gather all the bones of the murdered he could find. He buried them in a mound that stands to this day and was the village cemetery's very first grave. He succeeded in restarting the settlement but not as a place where Natives and White settlers lived side by side with a shared religion.

22

WAYNE COUNTY

Smithville

The village of Smithville, home to the excellent Pioneer Village Town Center, used to host to an annual Chautauqua, an event that was once quite popular in America that has since fallen into obscurity. In the early 1870s, a Methodist clergyman named John H. Vincent thought it would be a good idea to improve the way Sunday school was taught. Independently, and at about the same time, a layman named Lewis Miller had the same idea. In August 1874, the two organized a meeting dedicated to teaching Sunday school teachers new ways of instruction in a woodland along Chautauqua Lake, New York, the first meeting of this type.

Miller, a prominent businessman and inventor from Akron whose daughter had married Thomas Edison, cofounded, along with John Heyl Vincent, the Chautauqua Institution, with the mandate to discuss import religious, political and social issues of the day. He had implemented his own Sunday school reforms at the First Methodist Church in 1872. Another of the Chautauqua's founders started a school that taught Hebrew and Greek (the languages in which most of the Bible was written) and later added French, German and Latin.

Beyond training Sunday school teachers, subsequent meetings expanded into other areas, including teaching children to read and write so that they could better understand the Bible. In 1882, the Society of the Hall in the Grove, now known as the Alumni Association of the Chautauqua Literary and Scientific Circle, formed to promote reading. Those who

William Jennings Bryan. *Courtesy of the Library of Congress.*

completed four years of reading the Circle's list of works received a certificate. Members formed discussion circles that arguably became the first book clubs in the United States.

The New York Chautauqua's success prompted many imitators, all of which the original disavowed. Some Chautauquas traveled on designated circuits. From 1899 to 1916, Professor John B. Eberly ran a two-week Chautauqua in Smithville every August. At this point, politics had become a part of these gatherings, and William Jennings Bryan was one of the more famous politicians to appear at them. In Smithville and many other places, he gave his famous "Prince of Peace" speech, in which he argued that Jesus's message to the world was for peace. Bryan was, himself, a pacifist.

Born into a prosperous family in Salem, Illinois, on March 19, 1860, Bryan was a devout Presbyterian and, like his father, a lawyer. It is surprising how progressive he was, considering he ended his legal career with the Scopes Monkey Trial, in which he argued evolution shouldn't be taught in schools. The trial inspired the play *Inherit the Wind*, which was later adapted as a movie and numerous television programs. Bryan's wife, Mary Baird, was a lawyer in her own right and worked side by side with her husband in politics. Both wanted a nationwide ban on alcohol and, at the same time, advocated for woman's suffrage—the two often going hand in hand.

In 1890, he won his first political office as a congressman whose district included Omaha and Lincoln, Nebraska. Bryan was a superb orator, and it was his "Cross of Gold" speech at the 1896 Democratic Convention, in which he argued that the U.S. currency should be backed by silver, not gold, that secured him his first presidential nomination. He lost, but that didn't deter the Democrats from nominating him again in 1900. After losing this race as well, he turned to writing and speaking on the lecture circuits, including the Chautauqua ones. Nominated as the Democratic presidential candidate for a third time in 1908, Bryan lost once more and never ran for that office again, although he did pen much of the winning 1912 Democratic presidential platform for Woodrow Wilson.

It's quite possible that members of the Sheller family attended one of Smithville's Chautauquas. Their house, which now stands in Smithville's Pioneer Village Town Center, has on its first floor a secretary (writing desk) with a bookcase built by village cabinet maker John Zimmerman. He was born in Philadelphia in 1800 and was indentured to cabinet maker Daniel Markley of Cocalico Township in Lancaster County, Pennsylvania, in 1816. His indentureship paper is on display in the house.

Indentured servitude is sometimes compared to the enslavement of Black people as an excuse to say that White people were affected by this institution as well, but the comparison is not valid. In Zimmerman's case, being indentured was part of his apprenticeship. Once completed, he was not only free, he lived a prosperous life. In addition to making cabinets, he also constructed coffins, served as a justice of the peace and served as a notary. Enslaved Black people, in contrast, were considered chattel—subhuman—and few of those who earned their freedom ever reached the ranks of the American middle or upper classes. The children of indentured servants weren't born into that same state while those treated as chattel were.

Indentured servants of the type most know from their school textbooks—those who agreed to become a servant for a number of years in exchange for passage to America—were just one part of the system. Also forced into indentured servitude were domestic orphans, criminals, debtors and paupers. Parents who were unable to take care of their children sometimes indentured them. Those who were apprenticed usually served their master until the age of twenty-one. Apprentices had to obey their masters in all things and keep their secrets.

Some contracts included a clause that forbade apprentices from playing cards, dice or any unlawful games. Apprentices were prohibited from going to alehouses, taverns and gambling dens. They couldn't marry. Masters were required to teach their apprentices a trade, how to read the English Bible and how to write legibly. They had to give their apprentices sufficient meat and drink, lodging, a place for washing and meet their other basic needs.

The system was often abused, and although indentured servants had the right to appear to the courts for redress, most judges sided with masters. Mistreated apprentices were liable to run away. Between 1771 and 1776, half of the indentured servants who ran away in Pennsylvania were Irish, a group already disinclined to abide by English laws. It was easier for White runaways to go undetected than Black enslaved people because they readily blended in with those in power. The apprentice system, which was derived from the old medieval guild system, died out with the rise of industrial

Sheller House, Pioneer Village Town Center. *Photograph by the author.*

factories whose owners didn't want to take care of their workers if they no longer needed them.

Near the Sheller House is the Lydo Barn. It was built by the Downey family in 1840; their story is an excellent example of the changes Ohio farmers faced in just three generations. The structure was given the name "Lydo" by Harold Downey to honor his wife, Nita Lytle Downey. Charles was born in 1892, and she was born in 1894. They were married in 1918 and took over the duties of Downey farm, the third generation to do so. It gave them the means to support their six children, but it never made them wealthy. Devastated by the Great Depression, they sold the farm in 1939 to pay off their debts.

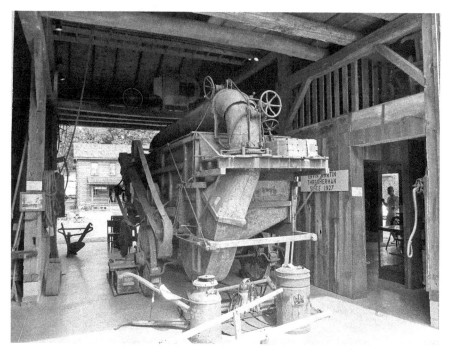

Inside the Lydo Barn is a thresher made in 1900 by the Champion Thresher Company of Orville, Ohio; Pioneer Village Town Center. *Photograph by the author.*

Both Charles and Ethel, the name Mary went by, only had eighth-grade educations, but they wanted their children to live better lives, and they did all they could to ensure that they did. After selling the farm, the family moved to Concord, Ohio, where Charles worked a series of jobs, including laboring at a strip mine, serving as the custodian of an elementary school and then serving as a custodian for a girl's dormitory at Muskingum University. Born in an era when electrification was largely confined to a few cities and telephones were just as rare, Charles and Ethel witnessed many significant changes. The automobile became the most important form of American transportation. The airplane, radio and television were all invented. Charles, who died in 1974, even got to see a man land on the moon. His son Harold later became the president of the Smithville Community Historical Society (SCHS), which runs Pioneer Village.

One block from the barn is the Church of God, the only building in Pioneer Village that stands in its original location. The Church of God traces its roots to Churchtown, Pennsylvania, where John Winebrenner founded this new denomination. Born in Walkersville, Maryland, on

March 25, 1797, Winebrenner decided not to work on the family farm; rather, he wanted to become a minister. To that end, he attended Dickinson College in Carlisle, Pennsylvania, until its closure in 1816. He then went to Philadelphia to study under theologian Samuel Helffenstein from 1816 to 1819. After being ordained as a minister of the German Reformed Church on September 24, 1820, Winebrenner's first posting took him to Harrisburg, Pennsylvania, where he oversaw the congregations of four different settlements.

His flock, disliking the excessive time he spent with the lower classes and his love for outdoor preaching and other innovations, had him removed in 1828. Undaunted, he continued to preach elsewhere. In 1830, he organized the fundamentalist General Eldership of the Church of God, with the mandate it was to be a place where the Holy Spirit could gather people to worship. In 1845, the church adopted the official but long-winded name General Eldership of the Churches of God in North America.

Winebrenner opposed the Mexican-American War, and under his leadership, the church became abolitionist. He was also a proponent of banning liquor—not always a popular conviction in the mid-nineteenth century. He chose not to run his church permanently and instead became a preacher at large. To generate an income, he worked in the secular world, doing things such as running a pharmacy and trying and failing to sell mulberry trees. He became a successful publisher of church materials, such as hymnbooks and a pocket New Testament written in German.

Some of Winebrenner's converts were lured by the cheap, fertile land to the west and eventually settled in Wayne County. The first gathering for their religious services in the Smithville area were held in the kitchen of Mr. and Mrs. Hugh Norris. The congregation built the Bethel Church in 1838 out of logs. In 1862, it decided to construct a more modern church in Smithville on top of land donated by Mary and John Zimmerman. This church was opened on December 16, 1867. By 2005, the congregation had shrunk to the point where it could no longer maintain the church, so it donated it to the SCHS.

BIBLIOGRAPHY

Museums

Ashland County
Cleo Redd Fisher Museum of the Mohican Historical Society
203 East Main Street
Loudonville, Ohio 44842

Ashtabula County
Jefferson Depot Village
147 East Jefferson Street
Jefferson, Ohio 44047

Carroll County
McCook House Civil War Museum
15 South Lisbon Street
Carrollton, Ohio 44615

Columbiana County
Salem Historical Society Museum
239 South Lundy Avenue
Salem, Ohio 44460

Cuyahoga County
Historical Society of Old Brooklyn Museum
3430 Memphis Avenue
Cleveland, Ohio 44109

Erie County
Follett House Museum
404 Wayne Street
Sandusky, Ohio 44870

Geauga County
Century Village Museum (Geauga County Historical Society)
14653 East Park Street
Burton, Ohio 44021

Harrison County
Harrison County History of Coal Museum (Lower level of Puskarich
Public Library)
200 East Market Street
Cadiz, Ohio 43907

Holmes County
Yoder's Amish Home
6050 State Route 515
Millersburg, Ohio 44654

Huron County
Firelands Historical Society and Laning-Young Research Center
4 Case Avenue
Norwalk, Ohio 44857

Jefferson County
Historic Fort Steuben
120 South Third Street
Steubenville, Ohio 43952

Lake County
Historic Kirtland
7800 Kirtland Charon Road
Kirtland, Ohio 44094

Lorain County
The Spirit of '76 Museum
201 North Main Street
Wellington, Ohio 44090

Mahoning County
Youngstown Historical Center of Industry and Labor
151 West Wood Street
Youngstown, Ohio 44503

Medina County
Northern Ohio Railway Museum
5515 Buffham Road
Westfield Township, Ohio

Portage County
Kent Historical Society Museum
237 East Main Street
Kent, Ohio 44240

Richland County
Mansfield Memorial Museum
34 Park Avenue West
Mansfield, Ohio 44902

Stark County
Spring Hill Historic Home
1401 Spring Hill Lane Northeast
Massillon, Ohio 44646

Summit County
Cuyahoga Valley Historical Museum
1775 Main Street
Peninsula, Ohio 44264

Trumbull County
National Packard Museum
1899 Mahoning Avenue Northwest
Warren, Ohio 44483

Tuscarawas County
Gnadenhutten Museum and Historic Site
352 South Cherry Street
Gnadenhutten, Ohio 44629

Wayne County
Pioneer Village Town Center (Smithville Community Historical Society)
180 Main Street
Smithville, Ohio 44677

Magazines

American Heritage
Atlantic Monthly
Confederate Veteran
Motorcycle
Nation
Southern Bivouac
Survey: Social Charity Civic
Trains

Newspapers

Anti-Slavery Bugle (OH)
Ashtabula Telegraph (OH)
Catholic Times (Columbus, OH)
Chico Record (CA)
Citizen (Honesdale, PA)
Cleveland Morning Leader (OH)
Cleveland Plain Dealer / Plain Dealer (OH)
Day Book (Chicago, IL)
Evening Star (Washington, D.C.)
Frederick Douglass' Paper (Rochester, NY)
Henderson Daily Dispatch (NC)
Mansfield News Journal (online, OH)
Milwaukee Daily Sentinel (WI)
Newark Advocate (OH)

New York Times (NY)
New York Tribune (NY)
Perrysburg Journal (OH)
Sacramento Union (CA)
Stark County Democrat (Canton, OH)
Summer Kent Stater (OH)
Washington Herald (Washington, D.C.)
Weekly National Intelligencer (Washington, D.C.)
Western Reserve Chronicle (Warren, OH)
Wheeling Intelligencer (WV)
Wilmington Morning Star (NC)

Databases

American National Biography
EBSCO: Academic Search Premier
HeritageQuest
JSTOR
Library of Congress: Chronicling America
Newsbank: *Plain Dealer*
Nineteenth-Century U.S. Newspapers
ProQuest Historical Newspapers: *New York Times*

Diaries and Letters

Esker, Anne. Letter from Esker to Ohio Homemakers. March 12, 1947. On display at Firelands Museum. Norwalk, Ohio.
Zeisberger, David. *Diary of David Zeisberger: A Moravian Missionary Among the Indians of Ohio.* Vol. 1. Translated and edited by Eugene F. Bliss. Cincinnati, OH: Robert Clarke & Co., 1885.

Pamphlets and Similar Short Works

Herip Associates. *Peninsula Village Architectural Tour.* Peninsula, OH: Peninsula Area Chamber of Commerce and Peninsula Library and Historical Society, n.d.

The Historic Church of God: Smithville's Oldest Church & The Oldest Church of God in Ohio. Smithville, OH: Smithville Community Historical Society, 2019.

The Underground Railroad: Escape to Freedom. Salem, OH: Salem Tourism Board, n.d.

Vischer, W.B. *History of Wellington.* Wellington, OH: Wellington Enterprise, 1922.

Government Documents

Adams, Richard C., and U.S. Congress and Senate. *History of the Delaware Indians.* Washington, D.C.: Government Printing Office, 1906.

Hall, Henry, and United States Department of the Interior, Census Office. *Report on the Ship-Building Industry of the United States.* Washington, D.C.: Government Printing Office, 1884.

Ohio General Assembly Joint Committee on Ashtabula. *Report of the Joint Committee Concerning the Ashtabula Bridge Disaster, Under the Joint Resolution of the General Assembly.* Columbus, OH: Nevins & Myers, 1877.

United States Congress. *United States of America Congressional Record: Proceedings and Debates of the 76th Congress, First Session. Appendix: Volume 84, Part 12, March 28, 1939 to May 24, 1939.* Washington, DC: Government Printing Office, 1939.

United States Interstate Commerce Commission. *Interstate Commerce Reports: Decisions and Proceedings of the Interstate Commerce Commission Under the Instate Commerce Act of February 4, 1887, and Amendments Together with All Decisions of the Courts Related to Interstate Commerce, with Notes: June 1888 to May 1890.* Vol. 2. Rochester, NY: Lawyer's Cooperative Publishing Company, 1890.

United States National Park Service. "The Jaite Mill." www.nps.gov.

Journals

Ball, Richard A., and J. Robert Lilly. "The Menace of Margarine: The Rise and Fall of a Social Problem." *Social Problems* 29, no. 5 (June 1982): 488–98.

Brown, Ira V. "An Antislavery Agent: C.C. Burleigh in Pennsylvania, 1836–1837." *Pennsylvania Magazine of History and Biography* 105, no. 1 (January 1981): 66–84.

Buck, Martina. "A Louisiana Prisoner-of-War on Johnson's Island, 1863–65." *Louisiana History: The Journal of the Louisiana Historical Association* 4, no. 3 (Summer 1963): 233–42.

Bush, David R. "Interpreting the Latrines of the Johnson's Island Civil War Military Prison." *Historical Archaeology* 34, 1 (2000): 62–78.

Catlin, George B. "Colonel John Francis Hamtramck." *Indiana Magazine of History* 26, no. 3 (September 1930): 237–52.

Clark, Dennis. "Babes in Bondage: Indentured Irish Children in Philadelphia in the Nineteenth Century." *Pennsylvania Magazine of History and Biography* 101, no. 4 (October 1977): 475–86.

Dupré, Ruth. "'If It's Yellow, It Must be Butter': Margarine Regulation in North America Since 1886." *Journal of Economic History* 59, no. 2 (June 1999): 353–71.

Enman, John A. "Coal Company Store Prices Questioned: A Case Study of the Union Supply Company, 1905–1906." *Pennsylvania History: A Journal of Mid-Atlantic Studies* 41, no. 1 (January 1974): 52–62.

Fishback, Price V. "Did Coal Miners 'Owe Their Souls to the Company Store'? Theory and Evidence from the Early 1900s." *Journal of Economic History* 46, no. 4 (December 1986): 1,011–29.

Flynn, George Q. "Lewis Hershey and the Conscientious Objector: The World War II Experience." *Military Affairs* 47, no. 1 (February 1983): 1–6.

Galbreath, C.B. "Anti-Slavery Movement in Columbiana County." In *Ohio Archæological and Historical Publications*. Vol. 30. Columbus, OH: Fred J. Heer, 1921.

High, Steven. "Deindustrializing Youngstown: Memories of Resistance and Loss Following 'Black Monday,' 1977–1997." *History Workshop Journal* 54 (Autumn 2002): 100–21.

Horsman, Reginald. "American Indian Policy in the Old Northwest, 1783–1812." *William and Mary Quarterly* 18, no. 1 (January 1961): 35–53.

Irvin, Benjamin H. "Tar, Feathers, and the Enemies of American Liberties, 1768–1776." *New England Quarterly* 76, no. 2 (June 2003): 197–238.

"Labor Agreements and Indentures." *Bulletin of the Business Historical Society* 8, no. 6 (December 1934): 104–10.

Marable, Manning. "Death of the Quaker Slave Trade." *Quaker History* 63, no. 1 (Spring 1974): 17–33.

Miller, Harry. "Potash from Wood Ashes: Frontier Technology in Canada and the United States." *Technology and Culture* 21, no. 2 (April 1980): 187–208.

Mills, Randall V. "Early Electric Interurbans in Oregon: Forming the Portland Railway, Light and Power System." *Oregon Historical Quarterly* 44, no. 1 (March 1943): 82–104.

Nye, Russel B. "Marius Robinson, A Forgotten Abolitionist Leader." *Ohio Archeological and Historical Quarter* 55, no. 2 (April–June 1946): 138–54.

Ousterhout, Anne M. "Frontier Vengeance: Connecticut Yankees vs. Pennamites in the Wyoming Valley." *Pennsylvania History: A Journal of Mid-Atlantic Studies* 62, no. 3 (Summer 1995): 330–63.

Preston, Emmett D. "The Fugitive Slave Acts in Ohio." *Journal of Negro History* 28, no. 4 (October 1943): 422–77.

———. "The Underground Railroad in Northwest Ohio." *Journal of Negro History* 17, no. 4 (October 1932): 409–36.

Pykles, Benjamin C. "An Introduction to the Kirtland Flats Ashery." *Brigham Young University Studies* 41, no. 1 (2002): 158–86.

Reutter, Mark. "Sunset." *Wilson Quarterly* 12, no. 4 (Autumn 1988): 72–83.

Sharkey, Noel. "Elektro's Return." *New Scientist* 199, no. 2,687 (December 20, 2008): n.p.

Skelton, William B. "Social Roots of the American Military Profession: The Officer Corps of America's First Peacetime Army, 1784–1789." *Journal of Military History* 54, no. 4 (October 1990): 435–52.

Smemo, Kristoffer, Samir Sonti and Gabriel Winant. "Conflict and Consensus: The Steel Strike of 1959 and the Anatomy of the New Deal Order." *Critical Historical Studies* 4, no. 1 (Spring 2017): 39–73.

Smith, Hobart M., and M.B. Mittleman. "A Brief Biographical Note on Edward Wilkinson." *American Midland Naturalist* 30, no. 3 (November 1943): 803–5.

Thornton, Harrison John. "Chautauqua and the Midwest." *Wisconsin Magazine of History* 33, no. 2 (December 1949): 152–63.

Van Cleef, Frank C. "The Rise and Decline of the Cheese Industry in Lorain County." *Ohio History Journal* 69, no. 1 (January 1960): 32–57.

Wallace, Paul A.W. "The John Heckewelder Papers." *Pennsylvania History: A Journal of Mid-Atlantic Studies* 27, no. 3 (July 1960): 249–62.

Wittmer, Joe. "The Amish and the Supreme Court." *Phi Delta Kappan* 54, no. 1 (September 1972): 50–52.

Online Sources

Alvarez, Anita. "Mansfield Memorial Museum Displays Elektro in Honor of Robot's 75th Anniversary." Richland Source. April 21, 2014. www.richlandsource.com.

Case Western Reserve University. "Encyclopedia of Cleveland History." www.case.edu.

Dell'Amore, Christine. "Florida Python Hunt Captures 68 Invasive Snakes." *National Geographic*, February 21, 2013. www.nationalgeographic.com.

Historic Structures. "FB Stearns Auto Company Cleveland Ohio." November 6, 2015. www.historic-structures.com.

Ishak, Natasha. "The Unbelievable Story of William Still, the 'Father of the Underground Railroad' Buried by History." October 29, 2019. www.allthatsinteresting.com.

Massillon Memory. "The Rotch-Wales Papers." Massillon Public Library. www.massillonmemory.org.

McKee, Timothy Brian. "Mansfield's Temperamental History with Alcohol." Richland Source. October 3, 2015. www.richlandsource.com.

Moravian Church. "A Brief History of the Moravian Church." www.moravian.org.

Motorcyclopedia Museum. "De Dion Bouton." www.motorcyclepediamuseum.org.

Radford, Benjamin. "Human Lifespans Nearly Constant for 2,000 Years." Live Science. August 21, 2009. www.livescience.com.

Religious Tolerance. "The Amish in the U.S. and Canada: Before 1900." www.religioustolerance.org.

———. "The Amish in the U.S. and Canada: Since 1900." www.religioustolerance.org.

Theautoera. "Jordon Motor Car Company." www.theautoera.com.

Wilson, Paul. "Dr. Carlos Booth and His Horseless Carriage." October 9, 2018. www.velocetoday.com.

Zulandt, Carolyn. "Jaite Mill." *Cleveland Historical*. October 18, 2011. www.clevelandhistorical.org.

Books

Baughman, A.J. *History of Ashland County, Ohio: With Biographical Sketches of the Prominent Citizens of the County.* Chicago, IL: S.J. Clarke Publishing Co., 1909.

Bellamy, John Stark, II. *The Maniac in the Bushes and More Tales of Cleveland Woe: True Crimes and Disasters from the Streets of Cleveland.* Cleveland, OH: Gray & Company, 1997.

Bellamy, John Stark, II, ed. *A Centennial Biographical History of Richland County, Ohio.* Chicago, IL: Lewis Publishing Co., 1901.

Bloch and Co. *History of the Western Reserve and Cleveland*. Cleveland, OH: Bloch and Co., ca. 1963.

Boone, Triplett. *Ohio and Erie Canal*. Charleston, SC: Arcadia Publishing, 2014.

Brady, William Young. *Captain Sam Brady: Indian Fighter*. Washington, D.C.: Brady Publishing Company, 1950.

Cary, Ferdinand Ellsworth. *Lake Shore and Michigan Southern Railway System: And Representative Employees; A History of the Development of the Lake Shore & Michigan Southern Railway, from Its Inception, Together with Introductory and Supplementary Chapters, Tracing the Progress of Steam Railroad Transportation from the Earliest Stages, in America and Abroad*. Buffalo, NY: Biographic Publishing, 1900.

Christiansen, Harry. *Lake Shore Electric Railway, 1893–1938: Fast Interurban Service: Cleveland-Toledo, via Lorain, Sandusky, Fremont, Vermilion, Huron, Norwalk, Bellevue and Intermediate Stations*. Cleveland, OH: [self-published?], ca. 1963.

The City of Detroit Michigan, 1701–1922. Vol. 1. Detroit, MI: S.J. Clarke Publishing Co., 1922.

Civil War Society. *Civil War Battles: An Illustrated Encyclopedia*. New York: Gramercy Books, 1997.

Clement, J., ed. *Noble Deeds of American Women*. Boston, MA: Lee and Shepard, 1869.

Cuyahoga Valley Historical Museum and Cuyahoga Valley National Park Association. *Cuyahoga Valley*. Charleston, SC: Arcadia Publishing, 2004.

Ellis, William Donohue. *The Cuyahoga*. Revised edition. Dayton, OH: Landfall Press, 1998.

Ervin, Robert Edgar. *The John Hunt Morgan Raid of 1863*. Jackson, OH: Robert Edgar Ervin, with assistance from the Jackson County Historical Society, 2003.

Fanebust, Wayne. *Brigadier General Robert L. McCook and Colonel Daniel McCook, Jr.: A Union Army Dual Biography*. Jefferson, NC: McFarland & Company, 2017.

Foster, Emily, ed. *The Ohio Frontier: An Anthology of Early Writings*. Lexington: University Press of Kentucky, 1996.

Green, Hardy. *The Company Town: The Industrial Edens and Satanic Mills That Shaped the American Economy*. New York: Basic Books, 2010.

Grismer, Karl H. *The History of Kent: Historical and Biographical*. Revised edition. Kent, OH: Kent Historical Society, 2001.

Hansen, Helen M. *At Home in Early Sandusky*. N.p.: H.M. Hensen, 1975.

Hardwood, Herbert H., and Robert S. Korach. *The Lake Shore Electric Railway Story*. Bloomington: Indiana University Press, 2000.

Heckewelder, John. *A Narrative of the Mission of the United Brethren Among the Delaware and Mohegan Indians, from Its Commencement, in the Year 1740, to the Close of the Year 1808.* Philadelphia, PA: McCarty & Davis, 1820.

Henes, Ernst L. *Historic Wellington: Then and Now.* Wellington, OH: Southern Lorain County Historical Society, 1983.

Hildebrand, William H. *A Most Noble Enterprise: The Story of Kent State University, 1910–2010.* Kent, OH: Kent State University Press, 2009.

Hill, N.N., Jr., compiler. *History of Knox County, Ohio: Its Past and Present.* Mount Vernon, OH: A.A. Graham & Co., 1881.

Hise, Daniel Howell, and Edwin. *The Hise Journals: A Diary of the Life of Daniel Howell Hise from the Year 1846 to 1878: Addendum Diary by Edwin Hise from the Year 1879 to 1883.* Salem, OH: Salem Historical Society/Salem Public Library, 2001.

Howe, Henry. *A Brief Historical Sketch of the "Fighting McCooks": Reprinted from the Proceedings of the Scotch-Irish Society of America.* New York: James Kempster Printing Company, 1903.

———. *Historical Collections of Ohio in Two Volumes: An Encyclopedia of the State: History of Both Local Geography with Its Descriptions of Its Counties, Cities and Villages, Its Agricultural Manufacturing, Mining and Business Development, Sketches of Eminent and Interesting Characters, Etc., with Notes of a Tour Over It in 1886.* Vols. 1 and 2. Columbus, OH: Henry Howe & Son, 1889.

Howlett, David J. *Kirtland Temple: The Biography of a Shared Mormon Space.* Urbana: University of Illinois Press, 2014.

Huckelbridge, Dane. *The United States of Beer: The True Tale of How Beer Conquered America, From B.C. to Budweiser and Beyond.* New York: William Morrow, 2016.

Hurst, Charles E., and David L. McConnell. *An Amish Paradox: Diversity & Change in the World's Largest Amish Community.* Baltimore, MD: John Hopkins University Press, 2010.

Kaiser, P.H. *Moravians and the Cuyahoga: Address Delivered Before the Western Reserve Historical Society.* Cleveland, OH: Mount & Co., 1894.

Kessel, William, and Robert Wooster, eds. *Encyclopedia of Native American Wars and Warfare.* New York: Facts on File, 2005.

Kimes, Beverly Rae, ed. *Packard: A History of the Motor Car and the Company.* Princeton, NJ: Automotive Quarterly Publications, 1978.

Kiple, Kenneth F, ed. *The Cambridge Historical Dictionary of Disease.* New York: Cambridge University Press, 2003.

Loomis, Linn. *Here and Now—Ohio's Canals: The Sandy and Beaver Canal.* Sugarcreek, OH: Schlabach Printers, 2000.

Lucas, Daniel Bedinger, and John Yates Beall. *Memoir of John Yates Beall: His Life; Trial; Correspondence; Diary; And Private Manuscript Found Among His Papers, Including His Own Account of the Raid on Lake Erie.* Montreal, CA: John Lovell, 1865.

Mitchell, W.M. *The Underground Railroad from Slavery to Freedom.* 2nd ed. London: William Tweedie, 1860.

Mott, Edward Harold. *Between the Ocean and the Lakes: The Story of the Erie.* New York: John S. Collins, 1899.

Nolt, Steven M. *A History of the Amish.* 3rd ed. New York: Good Books, 2015.

Ogle, Maureen. *Ambitious Brew: The Story of American Beer.* Orlando, FL: Harcourt Inc., 2006.

Perrin, William Henry, ed. *History of Stark County with an Outline Sketch of Ohio.* Chicago: Baskin & Battey, Historical Publishers, 1881.

Reid, Whitelaw. *Ohio in the War: Her Statesmen General and Soldiers: The History of Ohio During the War and the Lives of Her Generals.* Vol. 1. Cincinnati, OH: Robert Clarke Company, 1895.

Reynolds, David S. *John Brown, Abolitionist: The Man Who Killed Slavery, Sparked the Civil War, and Seeded Civil Rights.* New York: Vintage Books, 2005.

Saal, Thomas F., and Bernard J. Golias. *Famous but Forgotten: The Story of Alexander Winton, Automotive Pioneer and Industrialist.* Twinsburg, OH: Golias Publishing, 1997.

Schust, Alex P. *Gary Hollow: A History of the Largest Coaling Mining Operation in the World.* Harwood, MD: Two Mule Publishing, 2005.

Silver, Peter. *Our Savage Neighbors: How Indian War Transformed Early America.* New York: W.W. Norton & Company, 2008.

Skærved, Marlene Sheppard. *Dietrich.* London, UK: Haus Publishing, 2003.

Smith, M. Kristina. *Lost Sandusky.* Charleston, SC: The History Press, 2015.

Sterling, Dorothy. *Ahead of Her Time: Abby Kelley and the Politics of Antislavery.* New York: W.W. Norton, 1991.

Stevick, Richard A. *Growing Up Amish: The Teenage Years.* Baltimore, MD: John Hopkins University Press, 2007.

Stockwell, Mary. *The Other Trail of Tears: The Removal of the Ohio Indians.* Yardley, PA: Westholme, 2016.

Van Horne-Lane, Janice. *Safe Houses and the Underground Railroad in East Central Ohio.* Charleston, SC: The History Press, 2010.

Vietzen, Raymond. *Yesterday's Ohioans.* N.p.: Indian Ridge Museum, 1973.

Weaver-Zercher, David L. *Martyrs Mirror: A Social History.* Baltimore, MD: John Hopkins University Press, 2016.

Whalen, Charles, and Barbara Whalen. *The Fighting McCooks.* Bethesda, MD: Westmoreland Press, 2006.

Wood, Gaby. *Edison's Eve: A Magical History of the Quest for Mechanical Life*. New York: Alfred A. Knopf, 2002.

Woods, Terry K. *Ohio's Grand Canal: A Brief History of the Ohio & Erie Canal*. Kent, OH: Kent State University Press, 2008.

ABOUT THE AUTHOR

Mark Strecker has wanted to be a writer since he first learned to read. He also possesses a passion for history. In 1994, he graduated from Bowling Green State University in Ohio with a bachelor of arts degree in history, and he graduated with a master of library science degree (MSLS) from Clarion University in 2008, earning the latter, in part, to give him the skills needed to write well-researched narrative histories. Like many writers, he has had a variety of occupations, including selling appliances, running a toy department in a retail store and working as a graphic artist/art director at an advertising agency.

A native of Ohio, he has traveled extensively through the state. One of his hobbies is visiting museums and historical sites, about which he writes travel logs that are posted on his website, www.markstrecker.com. Some of his regular history articles can also be found on his website.

This is his fourth book. He is currently working on his next one.